Daring to be a Teacher
essays, stories and memoranda

Daring to be a Teacher

essays, stories and memoranda

Robin Richardson

ℓ𝑏

Trentham Books Limited
13/14 Trent Trading Park, Botteslow Street, Stoke-on-Trent ST1 3LY

First published in 1990 by Trentham Books
Reprinted 1991

Trentham Books Limited
13/14 Trent Trading Park
Botteslow Street
Stoke-on-Trent
Staffordshire
England ST1 3LY

Cover sculpture: Mobius Strip – Ancaster stone
by Neville Klein
Photography: David Koppel

British Library Cataloguing in Publication Data
Richardson, Robin, *1936-*
    Daring to be a Teacher: essays, stories and memoranda
    1. Teaching
    I. Title
    371.1'02
    ISBN: 0-948080-32-9

Designed by Trentham Print Design Ltd, Chester
Printed in Great Britain by BPCC Wheatons Ltd, Exeter

Contents

PART THREE: THE TEACHER AND THE LEARNER

PART FOUR: POLICIES AND PROGRAMMES OF CHANGE

MEMORANDA ON POINTS ARISING 187

Acknowledgements

People

The essays, stories and memoranda in this book are a reflection of the 1980s, and of two places in particular — the London Borough of Brent in the second half of the decade, and the County of Berkshire in the first.

Most of all I wish to greet here, and to pay tribute to, very many people in Brent — co-workers, comrades and colleagues in the education office, in schools and support services, in the community, in all the political parties. The book is offered in humble gratitude to all those in Brent from whom I have learnt, and by whom I have been inspired and sustained. It would not be appropriate, just here and just now, to mention anyone connected with Brent by name. In relation to my time earlier in the decade in Berkshire, however, and to places further afield, such reticence is neither necessary not gracious. I wish to record debts of gratitude to the following. I hope that they will not be too embarrassed to be thus mentioned, nor too dismayed by the disparate and eclectic company which I cause them here to keep:

Madhu Anjali, Waltraud Boxall, Shirley Darlington, Sarah del Tufo, Helen and David Dufty, Peter Edwards, Marina Foster, Audrey Gregory, Jagdish Gundara, David Hicks, Maurice Hobbs, Akram Khan-Cheema, John Lambert, Jane Lane, Pauline Lyseight-Jones, Mary Martyn-Johns, Berenice Miles, Susan Milner, Iris Morrison, Tuku Mukherjee, Chris Mullard, Mohamed Naguib, Chris Redknap, Jane Reed, Hari Sewak, Rashida Spencer, Hugh Starkey, Janet Stuart, Brenda Thomson, Veronica Treacher, Patrick Whitaker, Angela Wood, Norah Woollard

1

and Anne Yarwood. Of all these, I am particularly grateful to Madhu Anjali for aspects of the pattern and thematic unity of the book. However, neither she nor, so far as I know, anyone else mentioned here agrees with everything I have written. Certainly it is the case that inadequacies, failures and misunderstandings in this book are my own responsibility alone.

My gratitude to Gillian Klein, who has been an extremely helpful and supportive editor. And to Barbara Doubtfire; to Jonathan, Rachel and Ben Richardson; and, most of all, to Pauline Richardson.

Organisations and journals

Most of the items in this book were first written in response to an invitation to lecture at a conference or inservice course, and versions of some of them have appeared as articles in journals. I am grateful in these respects to the following: Bishop of Hereford's Bluecoat School (This Generation), Hackney Teachers Centre and *World Studies Journal* (Stages and Stances), St James's Church Piccadilly (Learning towards Justice and Memorandum to Oppressors), Social Education Association of Australia (The Age of Aquarius and What is a Lecture?), Bramshill College Hampshire (Bricks in the Wall), *New Internationalist* (Manifesto for Inequality and Truths about Bias), Atlantic College (Fancies and Fragments), University of London Institute of Education (How Learners Learn), Atlantic College and *Cambridge Journal of Education* (Talking as Equals), Ealing Community Relations Council and *British Journal of Religious Education* (Caring and not Caring), Walsall Education Authority (You Haven't Lost Yet Kids), the Language in Inner City Schools network and *Issues in Race and Education* (Worth the Paper it's Written On?), Cheshire Education Authority (From the Inner City).

Writings

Authors to whom I am indebted for their ideas, scholarship and pioneering are listed in the section at the end of the book entitled 'Notes and references'. Full bibliographical details are then provided right at the end of the book, in the list of works cited.

INTRODUCTION

1. Daring To Be A Teacher

Teaching is hazardous. So, behind and around teachers, and before and beneath them, is the world of educational administration — the world of planning, time-tabling, resourcing, allocating, checking, budgeting, appointing, employing, building, repairing, lecturing, training, advising, inspecting. This latter world is the water in which teachers swim, a theatre in which they perform and play, a home in which they relax and chat, a village or city in which they exchange and meet, deliberate and wonder, strive and stumble, struggle and succeed.

There is so much at stake. So much, therefore, is contested. So much, it follows further, is a contest: always there is a war on. Plainly, and most obviously, the futures of children and of young people are at stake: their lives and their liberties, and their pursuit and holding of happiness. Each child is individual and unique, of course, and has her own distinct unfolding. But also all are members of groups, collectives, communities: each belongs to a social class, an ethnic group, a religious tradition, a 'race', a gender, a local neighbourhood. Therefore the futures of collective identities are at stake in education, not those of individuals only. And it is not only the future which is at risk, but the present moment too: life, liberty and the pursuit of happiness this day, this week, this year. And further, you yourself are in danger — you the teacher, you the back-up administrator.

It can be that your very job, livelihood and future career become patently at risk, as a more or less direct result of conflicts and contests around you or beyond you. You may indeed actually lose your job. But regardless of material risk and loss, there are risks also to your personality, your own unfolding, and there is the possible loss of your integrity and humanity. As a teacher you are remorselessly battered by the pressures and pesterings of the young, and by their maddening oscillation, often, between mindless rebellion and equally mindless docility. You risk becoming loveless, bounceless, humourless, sexless, visionless — the very model of a modern (and, alas, of an ancient) bossy pedagogue.

As an administrator (headteacher, deputy head, education officer, inspector, adviser etc) you are not subjected to the same hourly battering from the young face-to-face, voice-to-voice, will-to-will. But you run even greater risks to your humaneness and humanity: you can insidiously mutate, with yourself being the last to notice (if, that is, you ever have the good fortune and the grace to notice at all), into a grey drained passionless automaton, perceiving and deploying other people as pawns, as files and functionaries, and failing to see them as the centres of initiative and decision-moulding which in fact they are, persons on whom you can and do depend, and from whom you can learn. You then do untold (in both senses — unmeasured and untalked-about) daily damage, through intricate knock-on effects and twists and snarls in vicious circles, to vast numbers of other people — to other administrators and to teachers, and then through these to kids, and to their parents and homes, their cultures and communities.

There is a poignant episode in *Petals of Blood*, by Ngugi wa Thiong'o, when the author beautifully brings together a complex range of aspirations and ideals, tensions and dilemmas, fragilities and dull realities. One of the novel's main characters, Godfrey Munira, starts his political career as a teacher in a village school. One day he takes his pupils out into the open air away from the four walls of their classroom. The subject-matter is botany, and Munira's purpose is to provide the learners with fingertips-on, vivid experience. He teaches the children the names of the flowers, and the names of their constituent parts... the stigma, the pistil, the pollen, the petals... and feels pleased and proud to be imparting hard, factual, reliable information. But the fragile social order between himself and the children, maintained by nothing more substantial than his factual knowledge and his academic language, begins to crumble when the children happen on vivid poetic metaphors to describe the flowers — for example they see a red beanflower as having petals of blood, thus giving the novel its very title — and when, noticing that some of the flowers are worm-eaten, they ask disquieting questions about why in this world beauty gets destroyed, and about why God allows it to happen. Munira replies that this is all a law of nature. But the children are not satisfied with this answer, and press him further with formidable questions about humankind, about law, about God, about nature:

> Man .. law .. God .. nature: he had never thought deeply about these things, and he swore that he would never again take the children to the fields. Enclosed in the four walls he was master, aloof, dispensing knowledge to a concentration of faces looking up to him. There he could avoid being drawn in. But out in the fields, outside the walls, he felt insecure.[1]

We many of us readily recognise Munira's dilemma. Teaching of science, we believe, should not be rigidly separated from teaching of politics, and neither should be sharply separated from poetry, metaphor, myth, metaphysics: the natural world, the social world and the inner world overlap and intertwine, and none of them can be adequately explored and learnt about in isolation from the others. Concepts of fertilisation, for example, and of growth, unfolding, blossoming, fruitfulness, decay, ending, new life — and concepts too of oppression, stifling, untimely death (eating, in *Petals of Blood*, is a recurring symbol of exploitation and political oppression) — belong to all. Further, education should be helping to change the world, to make it less oppressive and stifling, less unequal, and should be helping to build, on the contrary, greater equality and justice, greater and wider access to life and unfolding. We believe these things, and we believe too that learning should be through firsthand experience, through immersion in living and confusing reality, and through passionate reflection, argument and dialogue: it cannot be, and must not be, limited to places called classrooms, nor to didactic instruction by teachers, and deferential note-taking by learners.

But though we believe all this, we are time and again convicted by our own convictions — we do not in practice venture far or for long from the walls of traditional school subjects; nor, quite literally, from the stone, bricks and concrete of our classrooms and school buildings; nor

5

from conventional boundaries and hierarchies of physical/organic, humans/animals, masculine/feminine, fact/feeling, adult/child, teacher/learner; nor from the naming of parts and the hoarding of facts, and the chalk and talk, and the overhead projectors and worksheets, of traditional teaching styles. We do not dare to live and work with wholes. We prefer instead — not least, as in Munira's case, because of the hazardous tangling of identities and personalities in any and every interaction of teachers with learners — the security of fragments and walls; for example, and very typically, we prefer the security of, in Ngugi's remarkable and beautiful phrase, 'dispensing knowledge to a concentration of faces looking up'.

And as in the individual classroom, so in back-up administration in the individual school , or in local government. We have certain ideals about how human beings should treat each other and should relate to each other— the administrator should be 'person-centred' , we say, just as the classroom teacher should be learner-centred, with an optimistic and generous view of human nature, and a vigorous trust and respect for others. Good administration should be 'homologous', we say further, with good teaching — that is, having the same general shape and form, and being imbued with the same principles of effective communication and productive interaction. But in practice, all too often, we fail as administrators in these ideals, and we construct and manage systems which are fragmented not patterned, hierarchical not participatory, disabling not empowering.

All the items in this book, in one way or another, are about such dilemmas and difficulties — both in the daily life of school classrooms and also in the managerial and administrative tasks of headteachers, and of officers and administrators in local education authorities. The book's essential and recurring theme is the need for a synthesis between two main traditions of educational thinking. All too often these traditions are seen as separate from each other or, more damagingly still, as in competition with each other, or even in opposition. The one tradition is concerned with learner-centred education, and the development and fulfilment of individuals. This tradition is humanistic and optimistic, and has a basic trust in the capacity and will of human beings to create healthy and empowering systems and structures. In recent years it has been much influenced and strengthened by the new paradigms of wholeness being developed in both the physical and organic sciences, including in particular physics, biology, medicine and psychology.

The second tradition is concerned with building equality, and with resisting the trend for education merely to reflect and replicate inequalities in wider society of race, gender and class; it is broadly pessimistic in its assumption that inequalities are the norm wherever and whenever they are not consciously and strenuously resisted. Both traditions are concerned with wholeness and holistic thinking, but neither, arguably, is complete without the other. There cannot be wholeness in individuals independently of strenuous attempts to heal rifts and contradictions in wider society and in the education system. Conversely, political struggle to create wholeness in society — that is, equality and justice in dealings and relationships between social classes, between countries, between ethnic groups, between women and men — is doomed to no more than partial successes and hollow victories, at best, if it is not accompanied by, and if it does not in its turn strengthen and sustain, the search for wholeness and integration in individuals.

All the items in this book have in common that they are essays — and in both senses: each is a complete and fairly brief piece of writing and also an attempt, a trial, a foray, a probe. Further, each is in some sense a tale. Some, quite literally, are narratives, and nothing else. Many contain and are built round narratives. All have the quality of story in that they are conscious constructions from living and battling with sequence and consequence. And virtually all have in common that they were originally written to be spoken: nearly all began their lives as a talk, lecture, workshop paper or seminar paper. In virtually every original instance there was thus an audience to contain and entertain, to withstand and understand, to appear before and share with. There were obligations and expectations to observe and fulfil, and particular sets of persons, histories and circumstances, and affairs of the present moment, to attend to. On the surface, the original audiences for these essays were not as troubling or as threatening as Munira's children in the fields. But deep down the assemblies were very similar, communities of human beings whose searchings for order and pattern were fundamental, and who could not be staved off with hand-outs, or cabined and confined by rehearsed answers.

At best, a lecturer speaks with and for her audience, not to or at it. She takes leads, images and stirrings from her audience, and reflects back to them tentative accounts and explanations for events in their and her shared experience of causality. She and they together are searching for a narrative which tells a recognisable truth. The battle-stories and traveller-tales which she tells are like folk-legends: embedded in an oral tradition, and in collective, not individual, living and working. At best, in short, a lecturer is like a village storyteller at the evening firside. She is a spokesperson for the unfolding tradition, not its inventor.

Essays, stories — also, all the pieces here belong to the genre of memorandum, of notes to help the memory. They were written with precisely the same pens and keyboards, and at precisely the same desks and table-tops, as countless bureaucratic documents, jottings, letters, responses, agenda papers, submissions, proposals, applications, reports to committees, records, file notes, aide-memoires, and so on. And they were written with broadly the same range of purposes. In particular a purpose in every instance was to fix into memory a fleeting moment of reality: the memory of myself writing as much as, and indeed often rather than, the recipient. In fixing a moment of reality into the memory one is, at best, helping actually to shape reality.

My purpose in collecting the essays, stories and memoranda together and presenting them as a single whole is twofold: to pay tribute, and to provide a resource. The tribute is to those thousands of brave and daring teachers with whom I have had the honour to work over the years — learning, battling, debating, worrying, persevering, sometimes weeping, many times laughing, dancing, singing. You, my dear friend, you whose bravery is so awesome, you my comrade, you a brief but intense encounter, and you. There is nothing in these pages which I have not drawn first from yourself, and here now — yes, even as a village story-teller at the evening fireside — I return to you that which is yours, for your affirmation and heartening. For you may, perhaps, find here some useful resources ? This is my second purpose and hope. We live and work in difficult times, when precious traditions of learner-centred education and education for equality are under very considerable threat. Great daring is required of us. Resources to embody and sustain that daring are therefore required also.

To be involved in education, it is continually recalled and emphasised in these pages, is to be involved in politics and politicking — in jockeying and negotiating for power and autonomy, and in manoeuvres to resist the power, threats and intrigues of others. The struggles take place in the classroom itself, every day, every minute; in each school's staffroom, and in staff meetings, team meetings, parents evenings, governors meetings, the head's office; in the offices, corridors, chambers and committee rooms of the town hall or county hall; in contacts and combats between local and central government; and in the country, and indeed the world, at large. Several of the items in this book mention in passing, or imply, that as one seeks strength and courage to take one's daily and daring part in these struggles, one may find onself turning for inspiration to the fields of myth, metaphysics, religion, spirituality, prayer. There are at least five main ways in which these fields have implications for the daily worlds of practical politics.

First, political struggle is surely never really (though certainly it can seem to be) an end in itself: but takes place in order that the human spirit, in groups and communities but ultimately in each of us as an individual facing our own distinct frailties, failings, loves, pathways and dying, may develop and flourish. But second, whilst politics is not a be-all-and-end-all it is not merely a means-to-an-end either. It is itself, from a certain point of view, a spiritual battlefield where inner conquests of bitterness, self-pity, selfishness and fearing are more important than whatever outer territory is defended or won, and than whatever outer fruits are yielded.

For third, we shall be merely wearied and burnt out by politics, becoming cynical, manipulative, devious and intolerant, and with a paranoid conviction that our opponents are nothing but demons and monsters intent on our own destruction, if our inner being is not frequently renewed and nourished by art, myth, metaphysics, some sort of spiritual faith. Fourth, there is a point being made by Ngugi in the episode referred to earlier in *Petals of Blood*: Godfrey Munira needs to think through his position in relation to great metaphysical questions if he is to be able to cope creatively with the fragile social situation in his own classroom. For children, so long as they are children and are allowed or encouraged to be true to their nature, ask endlessly searching and unanswerable questions.

Fifth, the political animals within and amongst us are for ever bidding to co-opt to their own use and convenience the symbols and rituals which humankind has devised over the centuries to explore and to give shape to spiritual experience. Politicians, that is to say, all too frequently have a vested interest in neutralising the critiques and challenges of religion of any kind, and in recruiting religion to serve, on the contrary, their own causes. For religion can be so very useful, to give respectability to one's policies, and reassurance and a rallying standard for doubters. The cry of politicians, at all times and in all places, is that ' God' is on their side. This hopeful but deceiving assumption stands always in unending conflict with the forbidding awareness of the mystic, which is that God is on nobody's side, for she is both nowhere and everywhere. 'By whatever name you call me,' Krishna promises Arjuna on the battle-field in the *Bhagavad-Gita*, 'it is I who will answer you.' And Meister Eckhart said: 'whatever you say of God is untrue... I pray to God to keep me from "God"'.

The great myths of humankind have in common that, amongst other things, they explore the possibility of synthesis of outer world and inner world: of political struggle in objective forums, palaces and battle-fields and of spiritual striving in the inner recesses of the heart within. In mythology demons, monsters and foes of all kinds are both outside the individual personality and also inside it. So are labyrinths, forests, caves, prisons, and healing and wholeness, order and constancy, peace and freedom. At one stage in the great Indian epic *The Mahabharata*, the prince Yudhishthira and his brothers, at a time when they are exiled in the forest from active political life, are seized with a terrible consuming thirst. One after another they seek to slake their thirst in a lake in the forest, ignoring a mysterious voice in the background which warns them that they will even more certainly die if they do not first pause to think, to reflect, to wrestle with essential but massively searching questions. One by one the brothers try to satisfy their physical thirst rather than to answer the questions, and each falls down dead, until only Yudhishthira remains. He alone pauses before attempting to drink: he alone faces thirst in his own soul, as it were, before thirst in his throat — or before considering, for example, the political and social need for a reliable water-supply in society at large. In forcing himself to face the questions he saves both his own life and the lives of all his brothers. And he assures not only his and his brothers' return to politics and government but also the continued existence on planet earth of the whole human race. The sequence of questions and answers draws to a close as follows, with each answer wrung through intense and daring struggle from the deepest recesses of Yudhishthira's heart:

Voice: What is the cause of the world?
Yudhishthira: Love.
Voice: What is your opposite?
Yudhishthira : Myself.
Voice: What is madness?
Yudhishthira: A forgotten way.
Voice: And revolt? Why do humans revolt?
Yudhishthira: To find beauty, either in life or in death.
Voice: What for each of us is inevitable?
Yudhishthira: Happiness.
Voice: And what is the greatest marvel?
Yudhishthira: Each day, death strikes and we live as though we were immortal. This is what is the greatest marvel.[2]

Then the voice from the lake says, 'May all your brothers come back to life, for I am Dharma, your father. I am rightness, constancy, the order of the world'. The hope and persistence which Yudhishthira dares to utter are required not only of great mythical protagonists such as himself but also of real and humble persons located inescapably in precise history and in specific custom-bound circumstances, for example class-room teachers, and their back-up administrators. All the items in this book reflect a search for such hope and such persistence. All, that is to say, endeavour to weave together the outer world of political endeavour and argument with the inner world of private struggle, private search, private hope.

The original wording of the various essays has by and large been retained. But repetitions and certain topical or local references have been removed; criticisms by the original audiences have been taken account of and several passages accordingly expanded or revised; and some additional sentences and phrases have been incorporated, for example to make reference to the Education Reform Act and to other recent changes in legislation and terminology. Further, each item is introduced by a brief piece of connecting commentary, in order to give the book more coherence and continuity than it would otherwise have. By and large I have not referred to the specific circumstances in which the pieces were originally spoken or presented. Where, however, the original context is of relevance and interest, it is described — as with the speech at a school prize-giving, for example, and with the lecture to a captive audience of headteachers in one LEA. At the end of the book there is a section devoted to notes and references. The purpose here is threefold: first, and mainly, to give information about the sources of quotations and ideas, and to acknowledge a series of intellectual debts; second, to make some cross-references between diferent parts of the book; and third, to suggest follow-up reading.

All the essays date from the 1980s. As a collection, however, they are a resource for the 1990s, a decade which in British education is dominated by the implementation of the Education Reform Act. In many respects the Act is unfriendly and unhelpful to the assumptions about education underlying this book. Little or none of the documentation about the Act emanating from central government embodies holistic views of personality, learning and knowledge, and similarly there is little or no explicit reference to the need to address and combat , in and through education, inequalities of race, class and gender. Several of the right-wing activists whose writings over the years have prepared the way for the Act have made no secret of their resolute opposition both to learner-centred education and to education for equality. The outlook is in many respects grim, and is not helped by the fact that an enormous amount of energy is having to be spent on resisting the worst consequences and implications of the Act — energy which might alternatively be devoted to projects and endeavours which would be genuinely worthwhile. However,there are also exciting new opportunities in the 1990s, as a direct result of the Act. It is beneficial that schools have more direct control than in the past over resources; that each is expected to draw up its own overall plan for the threefold task of curriculum development, staff development and organisational development; and that each is more immediately accountable to the community in which it is embedded. There is no reason in principle why such greater autonomy and accountability should not provide the setting for major and daring new educational advance — for transformation, indeed, not just for mere reform.

Finally, by way of introduction, a word perhaps needs to be said about the genre to which this book aspires to belong, the collection of occasional writings. It is not, after all, a customary genre in education. Much more usual is the book of research and/or theory, with a clear unity of subject-matter and a consistency of formal academic style.

The apology for miscellanies in education would go something like this. Oh certainly there is an important place, it would begin by readily, indeed enthusiastically, conceding, for conventional academic books written from bases in higher education. There are however surely other bases too, the apology would continue, from which books about education may legitimately and appropriately be compiled — school classrooms and headteacher's offices, of course, and also, as in the present instance, LEA committee rooms, council chambers, offices and corridors. But if you work in a school or in local government you seldom have more than the occasional evening or, at most, the occasional weekend, in which to step back from the treadmill and the in-tray of your daily round, and to reflect and write. It follows that you can never write anything longer or more sustained than an essay, and that any essay that you do get round to writing is almost certainly going to be occasional in both senses: infrequent, and also in the sense that it is in response to a specific request or invitation, and shaped for a specific audience and set of circumstances. Such an essay may well be published in a journal, magazine or symposium, or in the records of a conference's proceedings. Nevertheless it is essentially ephemeral. Yet may there not be a case for ephemera to be given, sometimes, solidity and longer life?

Very much of education, after all, consists of ephemera and unrepeatable occasions. It is arguably therefore appropriate for a book to be compiled every now and again which ventures to reflect through its very form that much of our experience in education is ODTAA — one damn thing after another. But which reflects also that daring to be a teacher involves, amongst other things, daring to rescue and to treasure fragments and passing moments, and daring to get them and to hold them in wholes together. The writer inside each of us is one who carves and crafts words from the jumble and non-sense of a keyboard: not to write, says Philip Roth's alter ego Zuckermann, as he sits gazing down on the three nonsensical rows of letters on the typewriter before him, is 'to leave what is given untransformed, to capitulate to qwertyuiop, asdfghjkl, and zxcvbnm, to let those three words say it all'.[3] The task of the writer, when writing, is a symbol of the task of every human, reflects Zuckermann: 'to claim, exploit, enlarge, and reconstruct'. The daring which is required by Godfrey Munira, and by all of us in education, is exercised with your learners in or near a classroom and in back-up administration: and it is exercised too when you are alone reflecting and writing, choosing words and patterns, making wholes, shaping and asserting your ideals, and your reality.

PART ONE: AIMS AND IDEALS

2. This Generation
— speech at a school prize-giving

A school hall, an autumn evening, a cathedral city in the west of England, 1981. There were several hundred people present: all the school's teaching staff; all the governors; various local dignitaries; most of the pupils who had taken public examinations the previous summer and whose scholarly progress towards adulthood was now this evening being solemnly saluted; most of these pupils' parents, who similarly were both proud and anxious as they underwent a rite of passage in their life-journeys; and — sitting in the front row there, prominent in both his consciousness and his range of vision — there was the wife of the visiting speaker. The platform party included the headteacher in his academic gown, and the chair of the governing body, in his clerical collar.

The task for the visiting speech-maker was reasonably clear, though also — it seemed to me — unreasonably complicated: first, to catch and hold the attention of the kids themselves, and to say something both to them and for them; second, to provide a message of sympathy for and solidarity with the parents; third, to operate with seemliness within hallowed conventions and rituals, since the parents, governors and staff no doubt held these very dear, and would feel that their whole moral universe was under threat if there were to be a trespass against them; fourth, to keep faith also, however, with certain social and political commitments which were dear to myself, but which do not always or easily fit comfortably with solemn traditon and ceremony; and fifth — since our daughter Rachel belonged to precisely the same generation ('cohort', as schools say) as the young people in the audience, her seventeenth birthday imminent in the next few weeks — to signal some sort of message to my life's partner in the front row.

But come to think of it, perhaps all utterances about education — all darings to speech-make, to teach — have their ground in some such complexity. Be that as it may, it seems appropriate that this book should start on a ceremonial platform, and within the convention of dreaming dreams and sharing visions, and with subliminal awareness of my own family and household.

* * * * *

This generation began life, as all generations do, as babies. Life at the start for this generation was good, as it is for most generations, though not all. The food came along regularly, the mother's and the father's hands were warm, were gentle. These tots were cosy in their carry cots and God smiled gracious in his heaven.

From carry cot to play pen: this generation's infancy was bonny, bubbly, bunny, cosy, cuddly, comfy, daddy, doggy, fairy, goody, happy, jelly, lolly, lovely, mummy, nappy, neddy, noddy, pixie, potty, ratty, rolly, sonny, sootie, teddy, teeny, tootsie, veggie, weeny, welly, yummy. Everything, everything — not just Baby Bear's porridge but everything — was just right.

All you need, hummed and sang and gently danced this generation's parents, echoing the words of a song current in the early days of their marriages, all you need is love. Love is all you need. This generation was born between the first of January 1964 and the thirty first of December 1965.

During those two years Britain became a new country — or so believed this generation's parents, and their aunts and their uncles. Twelve years of Tory misrule, they said, came to an end. The fourteenth Earl of Hume was replaced at Number Ten by the fourteenth Mr Wilson. Everywhere chains were to be broken and lost, there was to be the white heat of scientific and technological change, there was to be great release of energy. John, Paul, Ringo and George got their MBEs in due course not just for their contribution to the balance of payments but because they gave, in 1964-65, a habitation and a name to the bright-eyed, lively hope and confidence of the women and men who mothered and fathered this generation.

This generation was at playgroup and nursery school, and as rising fives in regular schools, when the Beatles sang 'will you still need me when I'm sixty-four?' It was closing-time for the shades of the prison-house, and this generation was inside. Mr Wilson was sent packing in the summer of 1970 during (do you remember?) an epidemic of mumps amongst this generation. Three years later in the autumn, when this generation was doing topics and projects on (do you remember?) dinosaurs, Vikings and igloos, the people in Israel were celebrating Yom Kippur. The concluding ceremony on that day, Neilah, recalls how, many centuries ago, the gates of the temple were closed at nightfall, to symbolise the closing of the gates of heaven, the closing of history's accounts with each man, each woman.

As they closed the gates of the temple and of heaven that evening, a war started in that land. According to some calculations it was the hundredth war in the world since 1945. It finished very quickly but it led directly, two or three weeks later, as this generation continued its topics and projects on dinosaurs, Vikings and igloos, to the single most important event yet in this generation's lifetime — OPEC's decision to control from henceforth the price of bus-fares, of electric switches, of plastic bags, of all the foundations of this generation's daily life.

Members of this generation learnt things during their time at secondary school in the late 1970s — though, alas, they did not often learn these things formally at school itself — about which their parents, at secondary school thirty or so years earlier, had known nothing. They learnt about the Third World and about One World, about pollution and conservation, about torture and human rights, about Trident, Cruise and SS20. At the time that they were revising for and writing and recovering from their O levels and CSEs in spring and summer 1981, they learnt about some places in their own country called Brixton, Moss Side, and Toxteth. And they learnt that there were three million people in their society for whom there was no work, no use.

It was in the late 1980s and early 1990s that this generation found itself buying carry-cots and nappies, and books about Baby Bear and his porridge. Before marriage and children, though, this generation did do something about Trident, Cruise and SS20 and related issues. Oh, they weren't the only generation working on this, and they didn't solve all aspects of the East-West conflict. But they did play their part. And they played it not just with badges and banners but also through ballot-boxes and branch meetings, through politics and pressure in towns and villages all over the land.

Also after they were married, this generation worked on the issues of their world. They worked in particular on race relations matters in their own country, and on prejudices in their own hearts and minds. Non-European people, Rudyard Kipling had said to their great-grandparents about ninety years earlier, are 'half-devil, half-child'. No, proclaimed this generation — in strenuous political and legal action as well as in words — all human beings are of equal value.

If Black and Asian people are to have more power, both within this country and in the world generally, then white people must have less. There is no other way. If women are to have more power, men must have less. If pupils in schools are to have more power, teachers must have less. If children are to have more power — if, that is to say, children are to grow up into adults — parents must have less. There is no other way. This is what this generation knew, and this is what it proclaimed.

During the first decade or so of the twenty-first century, most of the parents of this generation died. They still needed each other, and still pleased and heeded each other, when they were sixty-four. But by seventy-four years of age, on average, they were not still needed by history. Their account with history was closed.

This generation was at the height of its powers from about the year 2010 onwards. Like their parents some thirty years earlier, this generation worked on the issues of their world — issues of conflict and power. And they worked too on issues in their families and private lives — these also were to do with conflict and power, and with the closing of prison-house shades, the closing of the gates of heaven, the closing of history's accounts.

This generation was all dead by about the year 2040. It didn't solve all the problems of the world, nor all the problems which it encountered in its marriages and family life. No generation ever does.

But it worked on those problems. That is why we today must praise, why we must thank, why we must bless, this generation.

3. Stages and Stances
— a tale with two parts

The educational air in the 1990s is thick with discourse of 'attainment targets', 'attainment levels', 'profile components', 'key stages', 'reporting ages', 'standardised attainment tasks', and so on. Quite a lot of this discourse shows scant respect for all existing dictionary definitions hitherto. None of it shows respect for the glorious untidiness and bloody-mindedness of real human beings. (Overheard, somewhere: 'Why did the government start the national curriculum with five-year-olds ?' — *'Because they think five-year-olds are particularly amenable and biddable and easy to mould.'* — *'Just shows how out of touch with reality the government actually is.')*

Also, the new discourse of the 1990s shows no regard for inequalities and injustices in society at large, or in the education system itself — *no regard, for example, for the issues and concerns which were put to 'This Generation' in the ceremonial speech printed on previous pages. There are indeed many reasons why the discourse should be criticised and, insofar as this is possible, resisted. However, a degree of structure in our thinking and planning about education is valuable and important* — *we do need to scheme if members of 'This Generation', and of each succeeding generation, are to develop in the ways we dare to hope for them.*

The story which follows presents a scheme which is very different from that of the national curriculum: its central concept is political and personal power, and it distinguishes the learning tasks of the power-ful from the learning tasks of the power-less. The temporal metaphor (1960s,1970s etc) is not to be taken literally: it does however help us to remember that education is embedded in history, as are the individual human beings involved in it, and to recall that there are respects in which our thinking about power in education and society has changed and developed over the years. Further, the temporal metaphor recalls that very frequently any one individual passes through these stances in sequence.

In a later essay the scheme proposed through this story is presented in a more analytical, more conventional format. But first, for the storytelling and storylistening animals amongst us, it seems important to ponder a narrative.

* * * * *

Part One : Davinder's Part

In the 1960s Davinder was content to conform to her world.

She had no rightful place in the sun, all rightful spaces were habited and managed by her father and brothers, by the great western energy which made her trains run on time, by the half-angel, half-parent who took up her burdens, by Eurolove Incorporated who cared and dared for her, drafted and declaimed for her.

She thanked God for her benefactors, and that he — and they — forgave her that she was herself stupid, clumsy, unorganised, that there was no wealth in her. She trusted fate and fantasy, the cool unending rhythms of the stars through the heavens, her dreams of perfection beyond the sky.

God's trains ran on time, and she knew her station, knew where to get off. Content to conform was Davinder in the 1960s.

In the 1970s Davinder reckoned to reform her world.

There were respects in which her master's world could be improved, respects in which she herself and some of her friends could have a place in the master's sun. She appealed to the better nature of God the Father, her petitions were heeded, she was full of thanks.

She wore this badge, Davinder is Beautiful. Researched her roots, husbanded her heritage, laid out her language, cultivated collections from her past. Was welcomed and appreciated by her elders and betters, pastors and masters, was full of thanks.

Lo it was good. Reckoning to reform was Davinder in the 1970s.

In the 1980s Davinder was despairing and defiant to deform her world.

The world was rotten through and through, had been tamed and named by monsters. Was run and over-run by evil. Foul and vicious, twisting and torturing, destroying everything beautiful, it had to be turned upside down.

No new initiative of any interest to Davinder could be expected of God or gods, from masters of any kind. No speech of theirs could save. Their patterns, plays and alliterations were poison, the only profit on their language was cursing. Let the world burn, for where else but from combustion and the molten do new worlds take wing?

Exodus: and a final plague on the old order. Despairing and defiant to deform was Davinder in the 1980s.

In the 1990s Davinder turned and toiled to transform her world.

She sighted a new heaven and a new earth without, and a new dreaming and a new reasoning within, and she knew that these would only ever come together, if they came together at all, in solid but sinuous spirals and circles. She spoke and moved not in anger or in envy but in love, which moves the sun and other stars. Listened to her comrades, did not lecture them. Organised craftily and artfully. Quarried and carved new ways, new words.

She found and forged allies everywhere. Loved even, and especially, the exhausted and the broken in her own ranks and files. Relaxed frequently, relented never.

World and word are hers. Turning and toiling to transform is Davinder in the 1990s.

Part Two : David's Part

In the 1960s David was content to conform to his world.

He had a clear-carved, clean-eyed space in the sun, and from the ground around him the fixed grin of the sun never faded. All roads, codes, goods, gods and tides ran his way, his tongue patterned creation, he had the whole world in his velvet-gloved hands: white was light and right, male could neither fail nor stale, west was best.

The world was his privilege and his pride, a reward for his good works, he had talent to manage. People not born to share the sun with David did not merit, with their quaint and savage and sometimes wicked ways, to come close to him. They were distant beneath him: half-devils, half-children, all of them.

God had elected him. Content to conform was David in the 1960s.

In the 1970s David reckoned to reform his world.

He knew that David/black, David/female, David/worker, David/ third world were not in all respects entirely adequate or accurate distinctions and, more to the point, not in all respects working in David's own best interests. Certain women etc were quite decent chaps really. He reckoned to groom some of them, and to admit them to a place in his sun. He counted on their thanking him, rewarding and repaying him.

And he favoured now the foreign — entered ethnic shops and markets, swooned to sitars, dabbled in diversity, consumed contrast and colour, patronised pluralism.

Lo it was good. Reckoning to reform was David in the 1970s.

In the 1980s David was despairing and defiant to deform his world. The world was bad, foul, pestilential, there was no health in it. He and his forefathers and brothers had made the world in their own image, they had battered and benefited, plundered and profited, were even now, with every step and breath they took, grabbing, grasping, gaining, getting.

The world had to be torn apart, he had to let it burn, for where else but from combustion and the molten do new worlds take wing? His vocation was to be cynic, spy and saboteur. Muddler, muckraker and mole.

All must descend into hell. Despairing and defiant to deform was David in the 1980s.

In the 1990s David turned and toiled to transform his world.

He reached for a new heaven and earth without, and a new heart and mind within. The programme was absolutely thorough change, of everything, everywhere. Woman/man, black/white, worker/owner,

27

body/brain, dreaming/reasoning, hearing/speaking, learning/teaching, nature/humankind: all these imbalances were to be dismantled, all these insidious circles and spirals were to be unchained.

He was to let go, let be, give away. Not in spite nor in guilt but in love, which moves the sun and other stars. To leave wells and other sources and resources intact, not poisoned. To speak and select with craft, not caprice. To empty himself, if he could manage it, with art.

Neither world nor word are his alone. Turning and toiling to transform is David in the 1990s.

4. Learning towards Justice
— notes for a framework

This essay presents conventionally and discursively the conceptual scheme which was introduced by the story of Davinder and David. It began life as a lecture at St James's Church, Piccadilly, and that same lecture included the piece entitled Memorandum to Oppressors *with which this book finishes. In many ways this essay, more than any other, is the book's key text.*

Much of our experience in education, the argument runs, is of unjustifiable inequality — that is, of injustice or oppression. The term oppression often seems unnecessarily dramatic, even melodramatic, when applied to contemporary Britain. It is used in these pages not to be provocative or dramatic, however, but because it yields two further words, oppressor and oppressed, to refer respectively to those who benefit from a system of injustice and those who suffer and lose. The term 'injustice' does not have this simple semantic convenience.

In different situations and milieux we are all of us both oppressor and oppressed, both David and Davinder — though some of us, of course, are most certainly more the one than the other. In both main positions we have a broadly similar choice of stances or orientations to adopt: between accepting the status quo as unproblematic ('conforming'); or trying to improve it a little for the sake of certain individuals ('reforming'); or trying to smash or deny it ('deforming'); or trying to change it radically and, at the same time, to change ourselves ('transforming'). At the core of the school curriculum there could in principle be some such theoretical scheme as this. More modestly and realistically, the theoretical scheme sketched in this essay can frequently provide useful insights, suggestions and reminders when we are planning or evaluating practical projects.

Very many of the other pieces in this book, it is worth mentioning and highlighting, are in effect continuations of, or illustrations of ideas in, this essay. In particular, as already mentioned, Memorandum to Oppressors *is directly related to it, and the essay entitled* How Learners Learn *sketches an ideal type of educational course concerned with addressing injustice, and promoting what is termed here, following the usage of Paulo Freire and his co-workers, 'critical' or 'transforming' consciousness.*

* * * * *

It's late evening one day in 1986, and we are are in the ruins of the Grand Hotel in Managua, Nicaragua. The ruins nowadays are a cultural centre, a centre of yearning and celebration open to the sky. Tonight they are filled with poetry-lovers. 'I do not think I have ever seen a people', says Salman Rushdie, 'even in India and Pakistan, where poets are revered, who value poetry as much as the Nicaraguans.'[1] The last poet to perform this evening — to share her words, her dreams, her defiance, her love — is Gioconda Belli, who has said that poetry is her political work for the Nicaraguan revolution. But for the moment, this moment, this evening, there is poetry not politics. Unless, that is, the shaping and performing of poetry is itself a political, revolutionary, transformative act. And so perhaps it is. Any way, 'rivers run though me', says Gioconda Belli, 'the geography of this country begins forming in me':

> Rivers run through me
> mountains bore into my body
> and the geography of this country
> begins forming in me,
> turning me into lakes, chasms, ravines,
> earth for sowing love,
> opening like a furrow
> filling me with a longing to live
> to see it free, beautiful,
> full of smiles—
> I want to explode with love.[2]

There is a remarkable fusing here of many different wellsprings and levels of passion, energy, commitment and delight — for the holy and vibrant land of Nicaragua itself, its very earth and skies; for the human body and sexuality; for comradeship, celebration and community; for social justice in every pulse and in every place. The struggle against international capitalism and domestic feudalism is motivated not primarily by a resentful or whingeing desire to end the old order, but by a passionate desire and determination to give birth to the new. And the new is characterised by producing, making, building, loving, growing, by taking a full part in the perpetual evolution and unfolding of humankind as a species. 'Real beauty is my aim,' declared Mahatma Gandhi from the midst of another of our century's great revolutions. 'The oppressed must realise,' said Paulo Freire from his work with liberation struggles throughout South America, 'that they are fighting not merely for freedom from hunger, but for ... freedom to create and to construct, to wonder and to venture.'[3]

What might a core or basic curriculum look like, or begin to look like, in an education system which took such concerns really seriously? That is, a system in which learners of all kinds and ages, and at all levels and locations in society's various hierarchies inherited from the past, were enabled to develop commitments, understandings and practical political skills for successfully building, and vigilantly defending, structures and procedures of social justice? This is the basic question to be addressed in this essay. It is of course an enormously grand and ambitious question. The response to it is inevitably therefore going to be modest, and to run the risk of being merely banal and an anti-climax. But long journeys start with single steps, and large canvases with small sketches. Here at least is something to expand, to enlarge, to enrich.

One modest place to start, in any consideration of what is basic in education and in learning, is a famous conversation in Jane Austen's *Mansfield Park*:

> 'But, aunt, she is so very ignorant!... I cannot remember the time when I did not know a great deal that she has not the least notion of yet. How long ago is it, aunt, since we used to repeat the chronological order of the kings of England, with the dates of their accession, and most of the principal events of their reigns!... Yes, and of the Roman emperors as low as Severus; besides a great deal of the Heathen Mythology, and all the Metals, Semi-Metals, Planets, and distinguished philosophers.'

The speakers are Julia and Maria Bertram, and they are talking to their Aunt Norris about their cousin Fanny Price. Their aunt comments, 'Very true indeed, my dears, but you are blessed with wonderful memories, and your poor cousin probably has none at all...you must make allowance for your cousin, and pity her deficiency.' Jane Austen's own comment is that despite the 'promising talents and early information' of the two Misses Bertram, they are 'entirely deficient in the less common acquirements of self-knowledge, generosity, and humility.' The whole novel can be read as an exploration and affirmation of these latter virtues, and of how they are acquired. Elsewhere in the novel the 'most valuable knowledge we could any of us acquire' is summarised as 'knowledge of ourselves and of our duty'. This is the knowledge, the novel implies, which should be at the foundation and core of all educa- tion : this is what should comprise, as it were, the basic curriculum. Necessarily, it includes knowledge of politics, of society, of power — it is a kind of political education not just, so to speak, a kind of moral education. Knowing your ABC, and other simple and 'basic' things, is not to do with cramming for success at Trivial Pursuits but to do with becoming empowered:

> Learn the elementary things! For those
> Whose time has come
> It is never too late.
> Learn the ABC, it won't be enough,
> But learn it! Don't be dismayed by it!
> Begin! You must know everything!
> You must take over the leadership.[4]

The relationship between basic literacy and empowerment was at the centre of the life-work of the Brazilian educator Paulo Freire.[5] This essay continues by recalling the conceptual scheme which Freire and his co-workers developed over the years with regard to the education of the oppressed, and suggests that it is relevant for educational planning not only in the contexts where it was first used — that is, in non-formal adult education in Third World countries — but also in school-based educa- tion in Western countries, and in the inservice and initial training of teachers. At the very least, it is in effect argued here, such a conceptual scheme needs to complement individualistic and apolitical schemes and models of human development, for example those proposed by Piaget, Erikson, Kohlberg, Jung, and so on. The essay proposes that much the same scheme can be used to devise an education for, in Freirean terminology, 'oppressors'. Since virtually all of us are both oppressed and oppressors in the course of our lives, and in the course of the transitions we make between different social groupings, contexts and milieux, the total scheme would appear to have very considerable promise as an aid to reflection and planning — both, to repeat, with pupils and students in schools and with their teachers in initial and inservice training. The scheme does not provide a core curriculum in its totality, but does stimulatingly sketch how a curriculum concerned with education against oppression, and on behalf of justice, might be constructed: it begins to propose what the attainment targets, so to speak, in such a curriculum might be. The essay is about theoretical aims and objectives, it should be emphasised, not practical pedagogy. A later essay, however, entitled *How Learners Learn*, also based on Paulo Freire's seminal ideas and practice, does go into details with regard to day-to-day methodology.

First, a brief stipulative definition: when a system of interactions and transactions produces and distributes more benefits and scarce resources for some of its members than for others, and correspondingly more losses and disadvantages for some than for others, then that system is *oppressive*; its beneficiaries are *oppressors*, its losers are *oppressed*.

This definition has three particularly important emphases or implications. First, it refers centrally to a *systemic* relationship between the winners and losers — they are not merely 'haves' and 'have nots' but are, so to speak, 'gets' and 'get nots', they are interdependent parts of the same social system. One person's gain is another person's loss. Second, the definition refers in principle to a wide variety of different kinds or levels of social system or social relationship: it can refer to a family or love-affair, to a peer group or team, to a school classroom or to a school as a whole, to an organisation or institution, to relationships between women and men, to relationships between 'races', ethnic groups and classes, and to the international system of world society. It follows that all of us, according to the different contexts and situations in which we find ourselves, are potentially both oppressors and oppressed. Third, whether you are an oppressor or one of the oppressed does not depend, in the first instance, on your own wishes, intentions or perceptions: it depends on your objective location in an overall system of gains and losses.

Freire's life-work has been with the oppressed. In this connection he has distinguished between four main stances or orientations which the oppressed may adopt towards the oppressive system of which they are part, and from which they suffer. His own words for these are translated from the Portuguese as, respectively, 'magical', 'naive', 'fanaticised', and 'critical' . The essential educational task, he maintained, was to move from 'magical consciousness' to 'critical consciousness', and to do so without getting waylaid by, and trapped into, 'naive consciousness' or 'fanaticised consciousness'. The four stances can alternatively be described with rather more homely and user-friendly terms, as in this essay: 'conforming', 'reforming', 'deforming', and 'transforming'.[6]

Within each stance there is a *problematique* with four components:

> **naming** (that is, a description of what the presenting problem is — of what it is which hurts);

> **reflecting** (an account of the background and causes of the problems);

> **acting** (a set of behaviours whose purpose is to remove, solve, manage or adapt to the problem);

> **valuing** (a vision of the ideal situation which would exist in the absence of the problem, and in the light of which the problem was defined and described in the first place).

These four components may also be summarised with the four key terms of 'problems', 'background', 'action', 'values'. Either way the relationships between them are circular and two-way, not — as implied necessarily by the listing above — linear. They can be shown graphically in a simple diagram such as the following:[7]

Figure 1: Problems: a framework for analysis

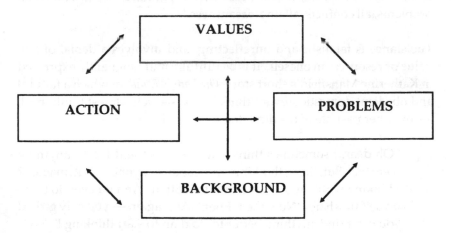

The diagram recalls and emphasises that action and behaviour always have three separate dimensions — there is the intention (either articulated or tacit) of solving, handling or avoiding some sort of problem; there is a set of theoretical explanations (again, either articulated or tacit) regarding the causes of the problem in human actions or in history, or else in fate and circumstance; and there are values to be achieved or defended. Similarly the diagram recalls that values always have three separate dimensions — they affect how people name and define a problem in the first place, how they then account for the underlying causes, and what they do, or don't do, to change the objective situation.

Putting together these two separate sets of fourfold distinctions - the four stances towards an oppressive status quo and the four components of a problematique — we can summarise as follows:

Conforming

This was the stance which Freire found to be commonest amongst the oppressed. His own term for it was 'magical consciousness', and this helpfully emphasises its non-scientific, non-rational elements. The voice of this stance goes along some such lines as these: 'Insofar as I am aware of any problems at all I'm concerned with survival — how to get through the next few minutes, the next hour, the next day, the next year. There is no particular cause to my problems other than fate and bad luck. And there is nothing that I myself can do to change or improve my situation — all I can do is hope for my luck to change, my prince to come, a miraculous saviour, a deus ex machina, a fairy godmother, a magic wand. What I desire, if you press me, is paradise — an end to all problems, all conflicts, all unpleasantness.'

The stance is fatalistic and unreflecting, and involves a denial of any value or resources in oneself. It is beautifully and poignantly expressed in Katherine Mansfield's short story *The Lady's Maid*, in which a faithful and obedient domestic servant thinks back — well, almost thinks back — over her past life of docility, deference and self-denial:

> "Oh dear, I sometimes think... whatever should I do if anything were to... But, there, thinking's no good to anyone — is it, madam? Thinking won't help. Not that I do it often. And if I ever do I pull myself up sharp, 'Now then, Ellen. At it again — you silly girl! If you can't find anything better to do than to start thinking !'"[8]

Reforming

Essential first tasks in Freire's educational process, it follows, are to give the oppressed a faith in themselves and in their own power and resources, and to enable them to think and reflect. There is a danger, though, that they will then interpret everything in terms of personal endeavour rather than with regard to structures and systems, and will be naively concerned only with 'making it' as individuals. The voice in this stance is accordingly something like this: 'I can see that not all's right with the world, nor with my life — other people have got more than me. But basically, I suppose, it's all my own fault — I'm simply not very clever or strong. Though I do blame some of the people with power, they ought be got rid of. So the solution to my problems is threefold — get a more positive self-image and believe in myself more; go out and improve myself, and get on in the world; and remove some of the individual people who are blocking me. I want a world in which everyone can get on and be happy if they really want to.'

The reforming stance was for Freire a danger to avoid rather than a stage to go through. He acknowledged, however, that development away from 'conforming' to 'transforming' might well involve being temporarily seduced by the naiveties of 'reforming'. Similarly he was aware of the seductive lures of the 'deforming' stance, one which is motivated by desires to smash and destroy rather than to build and create.

Deforming

This stance is common amongst the oppressed as soon as they have defined themselves as victims of injustice. The voice is angry, and full of curses and hatred. It may well lead to violent action, and this may well be, or at least will seem to be whilst it lasts, very satisfying. Revolution is the opiate of the people. Anger on its own, however, seldom or never provides motivation for the patient, gentle and unheroic works of construction and reconstruction which are required after the violence has been exhausted. The voice goes approximately as follows: 'The whole world is rotten through and through, and every aspect of my life is miserable. The sole cause of my misery lies with those who have power. They have been irredeemably corrupted by power, and there is no way that anything good can be expected of them. Least of all is it possible that they will give up power of their own accord, or co-operate with me in any way in the solution of my problems. The only hope lies in riot and revolution — smash everything, and out of the rubble, flames and chaos there may then come something better. Certainly a different system couldn't be worse. It's pointless and distracting, by the way, to speculate about utopia or an ideal future - the important thing is to put an end to the present.'

Destructive anger is more easily described than handled or transmuted. To refer to it critically here is not to deny its forceful reality, nor to imply that very major change in external structures is not required. The development from 'conforming' to 'transforming' must take the 'deforming' voice and stance very seriously, for it is to take seriously also the past, and the oppressed's own self-definitions and despair:

> This past, the Negro's past, of rope, fire, torture, castration, infanticide, rape; death and humiliation; fear by day and night, fear as deep as the marrow of the bone; doubt that he was worthy of life, since everyone around him denied it; sorrow for his women, for his kinfolk, for his children, who needed his protection, and whom he could not protect; rage, hatred and murder, hatred for white men so deep that it often turned against him and his own, and made all love, all trust, all joy impossible...[9]

Transforming
The goal of Freire's educational process is what he terms 'transforming consciousness', a stance which is concerned simultaneously both with very radical change of external social structures and with the creation of 'a new man and new woman', new forms of personal being and behaving. Descriptions of the transforming stance inevitably, and by definition, sound utopian and idealistic — unless, that is, it is recognised that the stance is a direction rather than a destination, a process to engage in rather than condition to dwell in. It is an aspiration, and is frequently, indeed perhaps typically, best described and commended through accounts of what it is not — that is, not conforming, reforming or deforming — rather than through direct exhortation. Instead or as well, it is perhaps best commended through story and metaphor.

At the risk of triteness and anti-climax, the voice may be articulated as follows: 'The society and situations I have been born into are unjust, and all people, including even those who appear to be comfortable and well-off from the present arrangements, are suffering. We are not realising our potential as creative, loving, knowing, feeling human beings. As individuals, as couples, as households, as communities, as institutions and organisations, we could all be playing a far, far fuller part in the gradual unfolding and evolution of life on this planet, and in the universe as a whole. But as it is we are trapped, trapped by the social and political structures which we have inherited from the past, and trapped also by our own cowardices, collusions, complacencies, betrayals and surrenders. But we do at the same time have resources inherited from the past — of love, of art and religion, of political tradition, of science and technology — and with these we can, and we will, build towards new power relations in many different spheres and at many different levels, and towards a new kind of human being.'

Indeed, the dangers are of triteness and anti-climax, or of utopian airy nothing. But at least a task for educators is being delineated. It is, as it were, to wield the poet's pen evoked in *A Midsummer Night's Dream* :

> ... *as the imagination bodies forth*
> *The forms of things unknown, the poet's pen*
> *Turns them to shapes, and gives to airy nothing*
> *A local habitation and a name.*

The transforming stance is not an orthodoxy, and certainly it is not a political organisation. Nor is it a developmental stage or level of consciousness which is ever reached and achieved once and for all. Rather, it is an orientation which is available in principle in every situation where there are unjust differentials of power, and which is available both to oppressor and to oppressed. But no tidy boundary can be placed round it, to show who exactly has it or belongs to it, and who hasn't, or doesn't.

Nevertheless some of the distinguishing features of the stance can be identified. The presence of these features implies the presence of the stance; and the absence of them, by the same token, implies its absence. But no straightforward match can be assumed to exist, between the outer signs and accompaniments of the stance and its inner reality. Five such signs or features will be briefly mentioned here.

First, there is the delight in physicality, including the natural world and one's own body and sexuality, expressed by Gioconda Belli in the poem quoted here earlier. 'As a rule it was the pleasure-haters who became unjust,' wrote Auden.[10] Food and wine, clowning and play, celebration and carnival, eroticism and conviviality — these are not sure and certain signs of the transforming stance (for, after all, they can all be engaged in totally joylessly and self-centredly); but their absence from a political programme, campaign or organisation, or from an educational course or activity, does normally betoken the absence of a genuine desire for transformation. Second, there is a genuine love for the oppressed, involving a readiness to learn from them, to live patiently with their definitions and perceptions, and to proceed at their pace.[11] The alternative to such love is a kind of manipulative or instrumental attitude, and this is sometimes found as readily on the political Left, in its 'deforming' stance, as on the Right, in its 'conforming'.

Third, there is a sense of interdependence — many different issues and places are seen as related to each other, and are therefore not treated in isolation from each other. Amongst other things this involves seeing and emphasising that there are many different levels of oppression, and that the same person may be oppressed in one context but oppressor in another. For example, in this respect, it is significant that in the description of Black American experience, quoted above, the viewpoint is very much that of men, not of women. Fourth, there is hope as distinct from despair, but also a certain 'negative capability', a readiness to live with doubts, failures, arguments, dissonance, questions, and with the partial expressions of truth expressed in metaphor and myth, parable and fable.

Fifth, the negative and destructive feelings associated with the deforming stance have been transmuted into positives. Energy is directed not into smashing and burning, but into confronting, opposing, arguing, campaigning, and into building, caring, loving, sharing, making. There is the energy of transmuted anger in, for example, Martin Luther King's famous *Letter from Birmingham Jail:* 'Non-violent direct action seeks to create such a crisis and foster such a tension that a community which has constantly refused to negotiate is forced to confront the issue ... there is a type of constructive, non-violent tension which is necessary for growth.'[12]

Freire's fourfold scheme was developed with the 'oppressed', not with 'oppressors'. But all of us have experiences of oppression — in our childhoods, our daily households, our loves and friendships, the organisations and institutions in which we earn our living. Even the securest and most sedate of oppressors can be plunged into experiences of injustice, or apparent injustice — through bereavement, through being dumped and discarded by a lover or partner, through rejection by one's own family and children, through awareness of one's own mortality and frailty, through insult and persecution on account of one's persona and location, not one's actual self. In all such situations there is a potential choice between conforming, reforming, deforming and trans-forming.[13]

But in any case the fourfold distinction also makes sense, surely, as an account of the stances which oppressors may adopt towards the unjust social systems in which they find themselves, and from which they benefit. They too, surely, can in principle and in practice choose be-tween (a) accepting their privileges and benefits as entirely appropriate and well-merited, and perceiving all threats to the system as intrinsically unwarranted and therefore as nothing but totally evil (conforming); or (b) having an uneasy conscience, and trying to make adjustments to the system for the benefit of, at least, a number of individuals (reforming); or (c) dropping out, with a paralysing sense of guilt, despair and emp-tiness, from all kinds of responsibility to maintain what is valuable in society and in the culture (deforming); or (d) trying to play a full part in changing both themselves and the social structures from which they benefit (transforming). These four possibilities were sketched earlier, in the account of 'David' in the story of David and Davinder. This is all by way of saying that, for example, men have a role to play in the building of gender equality; that white people have a contribution to make to the creation and maintenance of race equality; that middle-class people can contribute to the ending of class oppression; that parents and teachers have a vital role to play in the empowering of the young; and so on.

To summarise and draw towards a conclusion. Julia and Maria Bartram, and their Aunt Norris, had no self-knowledge, generosity and humility, and had no adequate sense therefore of 'basic', 'foundation' or 'core' education. They did not possess 'the most valuable knowledge we could any of us acquire — the knowledge of ourselves and of our duty'. An examination of the theoretical framework developed by Paulo Freire, however, can provide suggestions and pointers for the basic education of all, both losers and gainers, both victims and beneficiaries, both oppressed and oppressors. We need, and Freire helps us to develop, an

ATTITUDES TO THE STATUS QUO — TABLE ONE: STANCES AMONGST THE POWER-LESS

FOUR COMPONENTS OF POLITICAL OUTLOOK	FOUR TYPES OF RESPONSE TOWARDS THE POLITICAL STATUS QUO			
	(1) CONFORMING	(2) REFORMING	(3) DEFORMING	(4) TRANSFORMING
(1) DESCRIBING What is the problem?	EITHER — 'There is no problem'; OR — 'Survival, how to get through one day at a time...'	'We're not clever enough, not good enough... and certain individual oppressors are to blame'...	'The oppressor is the problem'...	'Unequal benefits and losses, therefore, injustice...'
(2) DIAGNOSING What is the cause of the problem?	'There is no cause, things just happen, it's luck, chance, the stars, the gods...	'The attitudes and abilities of certain individuals...'	'Oppressors never give up power of their own free will...'	'The whole network of structures and attitudes which we inherit from the past'
(3) ACTING What should be done?	'Nothing can be done, just hope for a miracle or saviour, a change in your luck...'	'Improve ourselves, take pride in ourselves, remove certain individuals...'	'Disengage from, resist, struggle against, eventually destroy, the oppressor...'	'Both structural and personal change — towards ever greater equality of work, power, wealth, esteem...'
(4) WANTING What is the aim?	'Paradise — an end to all our troubles and anxieties, an end to conflict...'	'Make the system work well — harmony, tolerance, equality of opportunity...'	'It is not profitable to speculate about utopia — first destroy the oppressive present...'	'Never-ending self-critical development towards new power relations and new people...'

ATTITUDES TO THE STATUS QUO — TABLE TWO: STANCES AMONGST THE POWER-FUL

		FOUR TYPES OF RESPONSE TOWARDS THE POLITICAL STATUS QUO			
		(1) CONFORMING	(2) REFORMING	(3) DEFORMING	(4) TRANSFORMING
FOUR COMPONENTS OF POLITICAL OUTLOOK	(1) DESCRIBING What is the problem?	EITHER — There is no problem (all's well with the world)': OR — 'Survival is the problem — trouble-makers, enemies of the state...'	'If people are poor, that is mainly their own fault... but certain individuals in power need to change as well...'	'The oppressor is the problem'	'Unequal benefits and losses, therefore injustice...'
	(2) DIAGNOSING What is the cause of the problem?	'Problems are caused by *evil* — evil people, evil power, plotting revolution, plotting world domination...'	'The attitudes and abilities of certain individuals...'	'Oppressors were created by history...'	'The whole network of structures and attitudes which we inherit from the past...'
	(3) ACTING What should be done?	'Evil should at least be resisted and contained... preferably should be stamped out...'	'Give people more skills and will to achieve... promote greater responsibility amongst leaders...'	'Sabotage the system from inside... or disengage from it altogether...'	'Both structural and personal change — towards ever greater equality of work, power, wealth, esteem...'
	(4) WANTING What is the aim?	'Security, order — an absence of threat, anxiety, conflict...'	'Make the present system work well — harmony, tolerance, equality, of opportunity...'	'It is not profitable to speculate about utopia — first destroy the oppressive present...'	'Never-ending, self-critical development towards new power relations and new people...'

ABC of learning for justice. Such an ABC is shown schematically in tables one and two. The overall argument can be summarised as follows, with four main propositions:

(i) Inequality and injustice are hallmarks of contemporary British society;

(ii) Education has a significant role to play in the long journey towards a wholly different kind of society;

(iii) Different educational programmes are required for 'oppressor' and 'oppressed', but these programmes need not only to be complementary with each other but also to have, in their shared concern to develop from 'conforming' stances to 'transforming' ones, the same deep structure;

(iv) Education for justice needs to be concerned with feelings and consciousness as well as with structures, and in this respect must forge ways of transmuting feelings of guilt, cynicism and emptiness amongst oppressors, and of anger and vengeance amongst the oppressed.

Later pieces in this book explore and illustrate these arguments further. Thus the essay on 'letterism', *Bricks in the Wall*, gives a fuller account of how an unjust system works in practice, using the algebraic symbols of X and Y to refer respectively to oppressors and oppressed. The essay on the Education Reform Act, *Manifesto for Inequality*, in effect suggests that oppression, as defined here, is systematically being enshrined in the 1990s into British legislation. The brief piece about an office party, *Accustomed As We Are*, recalls how oppression can be casually and ritually reinforced in everyday culture. The essay entitled *How Learners Learn* is then the second part, so to speak, of this outline of a conceptual scheme. It describes the practical pedagogy which Freire and others developed to facilitate the educational process of moving from conforming to transforming. Later in the book there are pieces reflecting attempts made in Berkshire in the 1980s to create and implement a formal policy on racial justice and equality, and therefore against the one particular form of oppression known as racism. The book ends with a private code of conduct for people who, through no actual decision or choice of their own, are beneficiaries of unjust systems. Entitled *Memorandum to Oppressors*, it constitutes an epilogue both to this particular essay and to the book as a whole.

5.The Age of Aquarius
— approaches for a dialogue

A purpose of education, the previous essay argued, is to contribute to transformation — the transformation of society, to make it less unequal and less unjust, and the transformation of individual human beings, such that they have the energy and the expertise to build and defend structures and procedures of justice.

The term 'transformation' is associated not only with political and educational radicalism but also with thinkers of, as the phrases are, the 'New Age' and the 'Age of Aquarius'. In a wide range of academic fields — including biology, physics, medicine, psychology, ecology, mathematics, philosophy and theology — there are new paradigms of wholeness replacing former dualisms of mind/matter, organic/non-organic, intellect/body, human/non-human, self/others, and so on. The notion that these various new developments all belong to a new age or new consciousness has been popularised in books such as The Aquarian Conspiracy *by Marilyn Ferguson,* The Turning Point *by Fritjof Capra, and* Man The Unfinished Animal *by Theodore Roszak.*

There has so far, however, been very little dialogue, let alone meeting and synthesis, between these two separate traditions which have in common that they both use the term transformation to conceptualise and summarise their goals. If such a dialogue did take place, what would be the main points which each partner would wish and need to make most emphatically to the other? This is the subject of this essay. In particular it notes the main criticisms and objections which the proponents of education for equality might wish to put to Aquarians. It closes, however, with a brief list of jottings which the field of education for equality might valuably take on board from the holistic thinking of the New Age.

The essay began life as a lecture at a conference in Australia. The theme of the conference as a whole was holistic education and its title, echoing Fritjof Capra, was 'The Turning Point — towards a new educational paradigm'.

The lecture began with a brief meditation on the nature of lecturing (reprinted here as a separate item towards the end of the book), and then continued with a traditional three-part pattern of thesis, antithesis and synthesis. I spoke at one stage about the place where I work, the London Borough of Brent, and about the outrageous attacks to which Brent had recently been subjected by certain sections of the mass media. All right, I was in effect saying towards the end of the lecture, I am prepared to listen to and learn from holistic education, and to take its insights back to my workplace, if you for your part will please attend, here in the apolitical warm sunlight of new paradigms and a new age and all that, to events and concerns in a tiny district of north west London on the other side of the world.

* * * * *

It is January 1919. The scene is a pub in the Grassmarket, in Edinburgh. Two young friends, both aged about 20, are meeting up with each other after the traumas of the last few years. They are talking about the shape of their lives, and are sharing their dreams for the world and for the century stretching before them. The one is John James Todd, who is later to become a distinguished film director. The other is Hamish Malahide, who will one day be a distinguished mathematician. John gives an account of his life in the trenches in France, and then switches the conversation : 'How's it going ? The maths?' — 'Incredible,' replies Hamish. 'I can hardly go to sleep at night. The things that are happening.' And the conversation continues :

> 'Astonishing things are happening, John. The most amazing revelations. Everything is changing. Science is changing. We look at the world differently now. We thought we understood how it worked, but we were wrong. So wrong.'
> 'I see.'
> 'I'll keep you posted.'
> 'Grand.' [1]

John doesn't know what to add. He says, 'Another pint?' and Hamish replies 'Yes, please', and the conversation ebbs gently thus to a close.

In effect, that conversation has been repeated over and over again in the course of the twentieth century. On the one hand mathematicians and physicists have been discovering and declaring that 'we look at the world differently now. We thought we understood it, but we were wrong. So wrong.' And the majority of the rest of us, as we listen to discourse of quantum jumps, wave functions, complementarity, probability theory, the uncertainty principle, the inadequacies of Newtonian laws of motion, the dissolution of either/or thinking and of the observer/observed dichotomy, have in effect been responding in the same way as John James Todd did in the Edinburgh pub. With a friendly interest, that is to say, in keeping the relationship open. But also, basically, with incomprehension: 'Another pint?'

The questioning and demise of mechanistic theory has found, though, a warm welcome in other sciences, including in particular certain branches of biology, psychology, medicine and ecology, and in aspects of theology and metaphysics, and the philosophy of religion. In all these fields there is an emphasis that reality is made up of wholes and interacting systems which cannot be described in terms of the properties of their constituent parts; nor described adequately with the linear, bit-by-bit apparatus of the left hemisphere of the brain. Both observer and observed, in the new sciences, are involved in a kind of dance. The archetypal image to evoke them is not a lone white-coated individual alone with arcane apparatus in a remote laboratory, in a remote research institute on a remote campus, but — it has been suggested, by way of vivid example — a moonlit rasamandala circle dance by the banks of the Yamuna, with the Lord Krishna flowing back and forth with ever renewed life and energy, loving, teasing and inspiring all of humankind in turn, and all at once.[2]

Paradigms of wholeness and interdependence from the new sciences have percolated in the course of the century into politics and economics through ecology and the Green movement, and through campaigns using terms such as 'one world', 'only one earth', 'global village', 'space-ship earth', and so on.[3] Also, and very significantly and powerfully, they have found ready echoes and resonances in the women's movement in many different spheres of social and intellectual life, with a re-emphasising of the receptive, intuitive, synthesising, holistic traits in nature and humankind, yin as well as yang.[4] Maybe, it has frequently been suggested, we are now at the dawning of a new age, more grandly of a New Age, as all these developments come together. Aquarius the water carrier heralds an end to dryness, an end to the deserts of rationalism, of dualistic either/or thinking, of mechanistic theories of all kinds, of macho 'mastery' of the natural world. Seminal books of the 1980s about aspects of the Age of Aquarius include three popularisations, *The Aquarian Conspiracy* by Marilyn Ferguson, *Breaking Through* by Walter and Dorothy Schwarz, and *The Turning Point* by Fritjof Capra. Other influential books include *Wholeness and the Implicate Order* by David Bohm, *Gaia — a New Look at Life on Earth* by James Lovelock, *Small is Beautiful* by E F ('Fritz') Schumacher, *Original Blessing — a primer in creation spirituality* by Matthew Fox, *A New Science of Life* by Rupert Sheldrake, *Eye to Eye: the Quest for a New Paradigm* by Ken Wilber, and *Dialogues with Scientists and Sages — the search for unity* compiled by Renee Weber. The following brief piece of doggerel pays affectionate tribute, though also rather ironic and disrespectful tribute, to all of these, and to some of the recurring terms and phrases of the new age (well all right, of the New Age):

An Affectionate Alphabet
-some letters for a spirit of our time

A is our Age, Aquarian, New
B's barefoot economists, and Buddhist ones too

C is creation, our original blessing
D's deep ecology, dependencies stressing

E's experiential education, extending what's known
F is the feminine, coming into her own — so

G is the goddess, and Gaia, and greening, and
H is life's holiness, and holistic meaning

I is intermediate technology, friend of earth and employment
J is jobs and real work, for cash and enjoyment

K is knowledge, knitting matter and mind
L is love, living Eros, renewing all kind

M's meditation, the motionless movement of the mystic
N's the new sciences, n-dimensional, non-mechanistic

O's the order that's implicate, Omega in time
P's post-positivist shifting to a new paradigm

Q is quantum theory, Newtonian physics dissolving
R's the brain's right hemisphere, reconciling, resolving

S is the small that is beautiful, and Fritz S of great learning
T is Tao, transformation, and the point that is turning

U's the unconscious (Jung and Gestalt more than Freud)
V's visualisation, a vehicle Jung employed

W is the wholeness of which all else is a part
X is therefore xenophilia, for the stranger an open heart

Y is Yin and Yang, but more Yin than Yang, and Y — my friends
— Y is you, and
Z 's the Zeitgeist I'm greeting here, but fearing for too.

Greeting and fearing: the doggerel is ambivalent, both affectionate and welcoming on the one hand but also dubious and sceptical, and a bit alarmed, on the other. The scepticism and anxiety will be unpacked here in due course. In the meanwhile let the greeting continue with some notes of exposition. The thesis greeted by the doggerel is that we are at the dawn of a new age. The sun is still low above the horizon, and at present its light is in pools, not everywhere. Here a lone tree is illumined in the dawn glow, there a hill, there a dwelling, here a small field..... the rest of the landscape is in darkness, and the illumined features seem at present to be unrelated to each other. When the sun is higher above the horizon, however, the various apparently isolated features will all as it were unfold and flow into each other, for they will be seen to be all part of the same landscape, the same climate, the same ecology.

Translating the metaphor — there are various trends in twentieth century culture which are apparently separate from each other but which in fact are nourishing and strengthening each other, for they all have much the same deep structure. The trends are related to each other as maybe the letters in an alphabet are related — haphazardly, accidently and arbitrarily, at first sight, but also, if human beings have the wish and the wit to combine them, as the building blocks, the coding devices, in a great explosion of communication and creativity.

Work to prepare and celebrate this explosion perhaps needs a manifesto, one which builds on a poet's dictum that 'the head and heart/Are neither of them too much good apart'[5], and which refers to other dualisms and dichotomies also. With a disrespectful nod to Marx and Engels, it may start with some such historic, well histrionic, declaration as this :

> The history of all hitherto existing society is the history of classification struggles— that is, of false dichotomies. Reason and intuition, mind and matter, animal and vegetable, animate and inanimate, mental and physical, cultural and natural, teaching and learning, adult and child, masculine and feminine, work and recreation, structural and personal, solemnity and play, in a word, oppressor and oppressed — have stood in opposition to one other, have carried on an uninterrupted, now hidden, now open, fight; a fight which could end in a revolutionary reconstitution of society

at large; but which may instead end in the common ruin of all contending classes.

To help conclude and to summarise this first section of the essay, here is an extract from a story by the Indian novelist Anita Desai. She is describing, from a university student's point of view, the final preparations and revision which take place before you take your university examinations:

> I felt as if we were all dying...that when we entered the examination hall it would be to be declared officially dead. That's what the degree is all about. What else was it about? We were ... pretending to study and prepare. Prepare for what? We hadn't been told. Later, they said, a BA or MA. These were like official stamps — they would declare us dead. Ready for a dead world. A world in which ghosts were about, screeching or whining, rattling or rustling. Slowly, slowly we were killing ourselves in order to join them. The ball point pen in my pocket was the only thing that still lived, that still worked, I myself was devoid of any more life — I mean physically, my body no longer functioned. I was constipated, I was dying.[6]

It is a beautiful description of how many pupils and students feel. We all of us remember the feeling from our own days as full-time students — though alas we continue to subject the young of the whole world to it. A new educational paradigm, however, would make learning vivid and alive, that is the thesis. Those whom the gods love, said Oscar Wilde, grow young. A new educational paradigm would involve children and teenagers, and all their teachers and administrators too for that matter, growing increasingly young. For it would be based on a totally new vision of human potential, both the potential of the species and that of each individual human being. In Brent our fundamental moral, political and educational principles are crystallised in the following brief and bold statement: 'All learners are of equal value, and have unlimited potential for development.' From the new sciences of the twentieth century, with their discovery and declaration that 'everything is changing. . . We look at the world differently now', we can learn in particular how to unpack the essential key concept of unlimited potential.[7]

Alas, however, it seems premature to embrace the age of Aquarius, and holistic education, with complete and uncritical enthusiasm. Some searching questions need first to be asked: the thesis has to be met with antithesis. For example, those of us who are involved in the practical educational politics associated with embodying the precept that 'all learners are of equal value' wish to ask, and need satisfactory answers to, questions such as the following:

TEN QUESTIONS TO HOLISTIC EDUCATORS

1. The Terms of the Debate
A basic seminal text for holistic educators is *The Turning Point* by Fritjof Capra, and another essential text in the canon is *The Aquarian Conspiracy* by Marilyn Ferguson. Both books have lengthy indexes — there are over 400 entries in Ferguson's and over 1700 in Capra's. Between them they have at least 1800 different entries, and it seems not unreasonable to look at these 1800 entries as a summary of their discourse, of their terminology and terms, their conceptual tools, their values.

None of the following words appears either in Capra's index or in Ferguson's: colonialism, discrimination, equality, exploitation, fairness, imperialism, inequality, injustice, justice, liberation, oppression, participation, prejudice, race, racism, resistance, structure/structural.

So the first question to holistic educators is this: are you satisfied that there are no gaps in your discourse, concepts and values? If indeed you are satisfied, what is the nature of your satisfaction? If not, what are you going to do about it?

2.The Political Right
What is your view of, and strategy in relation to, right-wing pressure groups and regimes around the world? You surely appreciate that there is no way they will permit holistic education to get more than a temporary foothold in the education systems and national curriculums which they control, or to be more than carefully cultivated and contained ornaments? Marilyn Ferguson says that 'all the king's horses and all the king's men' have never managed to change things. Well perhaps they haven't. But they are certainly very good at preventing change — as are, in Britain in the 1980's, the queen's horses and men, and at least one of

the queen's women. To repeat, what is your strategy in relation to the political right?

3 The Oppressed

In what ways are your programmes going to benefit the oppressed — working class pupils and their communities the world over; girls the world over; black pupils in white societies; children with disabilities and learning difficulties the world over; ethnic and cultural minorities the world over? In what ways, that is to say, are your programmes going to close gaps, reduce inequalities, remove discriminations, in particular discriminations which are covertly, indeed invisibly, institutionalised? And how are you going to win the trust of the oppressed? Which is to say, what risks — real risks to your material well-being, your career prospects, your reputation, your livelihood — are you taking? What boundaries of convention and courtesy are you prepared to transgress, what conferences, forums and arenas are you prepared to subvert, what comforts and friends are you prepared to lose?

4 History and Culture

Another key text underlying holistic education is *Unfinished Animal* subtitled *The aquarian frontier and the evolution of consciousness*, by Theodore Roszak. At one stage Roszak writes, 'We have learned that politics is a Chinese puzzle box: need within need within need: issue within issue within issue. Inside capitalistic industrial development . . . find liberal reform; inside liberal reform, social democracy; inside social democracy, personal fulfilment; inside personal fulfilment, the transpersonal quest.' That really is amazingly, if the word exists, occidentocentric — Western-centred. It complacently sees European culture in general, and Californian culture in particular, as apexes of human history and achievement. There is little or no real and sustained sense in the sourcebooks of holistic education, that non-Western cultures have known for centuries, indeed for millennia, about wholeness, about interdependence, about the holiness of all nature, both animate and inanimate. There are plenty of idealistic references, certainly, to 'ancient wisdom' and 'the wisdom of the East' and all that, but no recognition of the difficulties and obstacles which stand in the way of Western people learning from the rest of the world, both past and present — that is, difficulties and obstacles which have their roots in racism, colonialism and imperialism.

The question is: do you agree that you are unnecessarily Western-centred, and inadequately open to other cultures and traditions? If so, what are you going to do about it?

5 The feminine - and power and participation

There is much reference in the holistic education literature to affirming the 'feminine principle' in personality and living. Yes, but amongst other things this has to be structurally supported with changes not only in formal laws and statutes but also in unwritten rules, and in procedures, practices and customs. What is your policy and strategy here?

6 Vested Interests

You say you want wholeness, not fragmentation. You do realize, though, that the dichotomies which you say are false are not just inside people's heads, and are not simply going to go away because someone points out that they are there? On the contrary, they are institutionalised in all sorts of structures and career patterns, and very many people have a material interest in fragmentation and false dichotomies, and depend enormously for their emotional security and identity, and indeed for what they believe is their very sanity, on fragmentation and false dichotomies. What are you going to do about this?

7 Achievement

You don't want to go back to basics, you say, you don't want traditional examinations, you don't want undue emphasis on factual knowledge and rote-learning, nor do you want undue emphasis on the brain's left hemisphere. Fair enough, but you do appreciate that the children and young people who hitherto have been disadvantaged by educational systems do need, very definitely, formal educational qualifications? They need success in the present system, and therefore the minimum basic resources and skills with which to enter competitions. Are you confident that holistic education really will benefit, in hard, material and financial terms, the young people and communities who in the past have been disadvantaged?

8 Language

A historic task of education is to develop literacy and articulacy — the capacity to use words in order not merely to 'communicate', and not merely to shape and create meaning, but also to compose and unfold personal identity and power. Therefore, further, to assert and to protect identity, and to help fashion and control social institutions and situations. For the benefit hopefully of, but to the possible disadvantage alas of, other people. Articulacy and literacy — are you confident that you are developing these, particularly in children and communities who historically have been tongueless?

9 The conferences which you attend

Are you confident that the conferences, forums and meeting-grounds which you attend are constructed such as to facilitate real debate, real action, real change? That is, confident not only about the formal agenda but also about the format, and about the extent to which principles of equality, participation and respect for persons are built into, and reflected and expressed by, the structures and procedures? When you are not thus confident, what do you do about it? Are you a conformist? A drop-out or truant? A subversive or rebel? A reformer? A transformer?[8]

10 The grounds of your hope

What are the grounds of your hope? In an autobiographical memoir, the black American writer Maya Angelou describes a visit to a West African country, and an encounter with some villagers she feels certain are descended from the same pre-slave-age community as herself. As it were she is meeting, after 200 years, with her sisters and brothers. The meeting gives her a kind of peak experience, a mystical experience. She describes it like this:

> I was weeping with a curious joy. Despite the murder, rape and suicides, we had survived. The middle passage and the auction block had not erased us. Not humiliations, nor lynchings, nor individual cruelties, nor collective oppression, had been able to eradicate us from the earth. We had come through despite our ignorance and gullibility, and despite the ignorance and rapacious greed of our assailants. There was much to cry for, much to mourn. But in my heart I felt exalted because there was so much to celebrate. Although separated from our language, our families and customs, we had dared to continue to live . . . Through the centuries of despair and desolation we had been creative, because we had faced down death by daring to hope.[8]

The question is this: what experiences of your own do you have which enable you to empathise with, and to draw nourishment and inspiration from, the struggles of the oppressed?

Finally, and quite briefly now, this essay moves towards synthesis. The key word here is 'towards'. It is incidently a delightful blessing, in the English language, that the centre of 'towards' spells 'war'. You can't get to synthesis, or even indeed towards it, without the pains of disagreement and conflict, the pains of taking sides, acquiring allies you didn't want, losing dear friends you did want, being isolated, vulnerable, on your own. Be that as it may, here is a brief piece of writing entitled 'A memorandum to take home'. My purpose is to summarise succinctly some of the main things to be learnt from holistic education by anyone who identifies with the doubts, questions and criticisms sketched here earlier, in the ten questions. As it were, I am offering a kind of negotiation: if you can give me satisfactory answers to those ten questions, I am saying, then I am prepared to take back to my workplace some emphases from the world of holistic education.

It seems fitting that the points should be expressed largely in the shorthand of images and metaphors.

A MEMORANDUM TO TAKE HOME

1. Questions
Never stop asking unanswerable questions. What is the sound of one hand clapping? Which comes first — personal change or structural?

2. Avoiding Burnout
You have a duty to take care of yourself, and your self includes your body (for the body is not just that thing which carries your head around), and also your spirit (which is not just that strange place you sometimes visit, without being adequately consulted, in your dreams).

3. Diversity is a Value
Let a thousand powers loom, a thousand gadflies bite, a thousand micro-climates flow.

4. Suffer the Little Ones
The periphery is beautiful, small is reliable. Small may be trusted, cherished, nourished.

5. Images are Reality
In the shaping of images of our being, of our world, of our being-in-the-world, we are part of evolution's creativity and unfolding, we are shaping evolution itself.

6. Good Places for Kids
Schools can be arenas for the unfolding of selves — of bodies, of souls. Bureaucracies too. They are not inherently destructive, not embarrassingly irrelevant. Schools are good places, though not the only good places, on earth to be.

7. Say Yes
Cherish what you touch, love where you tread, embrace and delight in the person you are with.

8. Nothing Ever Finishes
Unfolding is endless. A millennium doesn't finish, nor does a culture, nor a project, nor a life, nor a love, nor a conference, nor a lecture, nor an essay. Everything, everything everywhere, is always unfini

PART TWO: CONTEXTS AND REALITIES

6. Bricks in the Wall
— markings for an inventory

The previous pieces have argued in their various ways that an aim of education is to contribute to 'transformation' — of individuals, of institutions, of society at large. The next few pieces describe some of the systems and patterns of organisation which need to be transformed, and the contexts in which efforts to develop and defend new kinds of education have to be made.

This essay on systemic circles and spirals of disadvantage uses an extended metaphor to refer, again, to two main sets of people: the sets who were named as David and Davinder in one piece, and as oppressor and oppressed in another. Here they are referred to algebraically, as X and Y. The purpose is to recall some of the complex ways in which the oppression of Ys by Xs (in a word, letterism) happens in practice. The account is hopefully not simplistic (though certainly it does run this danger) and not merely demoralising. It implies a whole package of measures which need to be undertaken in individual schools and LEAs, and indeed in individual classrooms. Such measures are described in detail in later items in this book — for example the essays How Learners Learn *and* Talking As Equals *describe ways of addressing and dismantling letterism in the day-to day-life of school classrooms, and the essay entitled* You Haven't Lost Yet Kids *recalls some key management tasks, in relation to letterism and letter equality, for headteachers.*

The other pieces in this main section of the book are respectively as follows: the piece on the Education Reform Act (Manifesto for Inequality) recalls the national context in which letterism is currently being supported, and indeed encouraged, by central government; the piece on an office-party (Accustomed As We Are) recalls that everyday, taken-for-granted customs and rituals in an organisation provide occasions for letterism to be continually rehearsed and consolidated; and the piece on fragmentation in cross-curricular campaigns (Fancies and Fragments) recalls that action against letterism has to be skilfully co-ordinated and organised, with many patient alliances and coalitions, rather than left to separate single-issue lobbies and campaigns.

There is certainly a danger, in using this playful and perhaps gimmicky construct of letterism, of trivialising real injustice. Particularly for the victims, injustice and discrimination are not laughing matters, nor matters for playful manipulation of algebraic symbols. Sometimes, however, indirect metaphors about injustice have a valuable purpose. The archetypal example of a metaphor about injustice is the tale of King David and the prophet Nathan: Nathan tells a story about a man perpetrating an injustice; David is filled with anger — 'As the Lord liveth, the man that hath done this thing shall surely die'; but since the story was in fact a fictionalised and disguised account of an action by David himself, Nathan delivers a punch-line which has echoed with shattering force down the centuries — 'Thou art the man'. In the very nature of things, injustice is invisible to certain people, in particular of course to those who benefit from it or collude with it, and only some kind of new and surprising metaphor may, perhaps, enable their eyes to be opened. So, anyway, is the justification intended for this particular play to catch the conscience.

* * * * *

A fascist who is nothing but a fascist,' wrote the Austrian poet Erich Fried, 'is nothing but a fascist. But an anti-fascist who is nothing but an anti-fascist is not an anti-fascist.' His point can be readily adapted to other campaigns and struggles: for example, an anti-racist who is nothing but an anti-racist is not an anti-racist.

Fried is making three highly important emphases. First, we need to steer clear, and to be seen to be steering clear, of mere sloganising and rhetorical shorthand; otherwise we invite jibes from the New Right and the tabloid press that we are loony; or that we are doctrinaire and authoritarian; or that we are merely a contingent of rent-a-crowd, with no carefully thought policies, and no precise language with which to commend or defend them. Second, we need to be as clear-eyed and as clear-speaking as possible about positive goals and values, not only about those things we criticise and oppose; we need, for example, terms such as 'race equality' or 'racial justice' rather than 'anti-racism' to summarise our concerns, and we need to be able to describe these goals not only as ideals to aim for in a distant future but also in terms of very precise, measurable, concrete, short-term objectives. Third, we need to be working for certain other goals also, simultaneously and as integral part-and-parcel of the same campaign; for race equality is not a 'single issue', and cannot be achieved without certain other things being achieved also — greater gender and class equality are obvious examples, as are genuine learner-centred education in schools and classrooms, and humanistic approaches to educational management and administration.[1]

This essay aims to respond positively to Erich Fried's three main challenges, and in particular to go beyond rhetoric and shorthand. This is especially important at a time when the tabloid press and certain right-wing politicians have succeeded in ridiculing the concepts and values of anti-racism and in implying that the concepts and ideals are espoused only by people with closed or underdeveloped minds.

Where to begin? One possible place is with the following brief piece of writing, which was originally devised for use with school governors in training about their new responsibilities for staff appointments and staff development, but which has also proved valuable for raising other, broader issues to do with educational customs and procedures:

Strange, wasn't it ? There were these two teachers, they had so much in common. Born on the same day, educated at the same school. Went to the same college, and both got distinctions in their teacher training. Started their careers on the same day, and at the same school.

The only small difference between them was that the one was an Exe whereas the other was a Wye.

Strange, wasn't it, that all the senior staff at the school were Exes. These senior Exes took a warm and friendly interest in the young Exe teacher, gave lots of moral support and practical tips, and lots of smiles and encouragement. This is what you have to do, they said, to catch the headteacher's attention, this is how to act, how to perform. The young Wye teacher, however, found the senior staff all rather aloof and frosty. Strange.

About three years later, an exciting day for the young Exe. 'You're loyal, you're hardworking, you keep good discipline, your performance is splendid, I'm giving you promotion. ' The headteacher speaking. 'Congratulations.'

The Wye teacher, in contrast, just isn't very ambitious, thought the headteacher.

A few years later the Exe applied for a deputy headship. Strange, that all the members of the shortlisting and interviewing panel were Exes. But since all the interviewers were Exes, the Exe teacher felt relaxed and confident at the interviews, and performed well, and was appointed. It's a pity in some ways, isn't it, said one of the the selection panel, that we get so few applications from Wyes, and that most Wyes perform so badly at interviews. Still, we've got to appoint the best candidate, haven't we. All the best performers are Exes, strange, isn't it.

And then in due course the Exe was appointed headteacher of a prestigious school. About half the staff at this school, by the way, and well over half the pupils, were Wyes. Strange, wasn't it ?

Certain issues are so important that it is not foolhardy to run the risk of over-stating them or over-simplifying them. This story of the Exe teacher and the Wye teacher, for example, certainly seems at first sight to be extremely simplistic. Nevertheless it can be used to illustrate a number of significant points about the whole field of equality and equal opportunities. Six main points will be considered here.

The first few are to do with the implementation of equal opportunities policies on recruitment, promotions and appointments. First, the story notes that the young Exe teacher's first step up the formal promotion ladder is through patronage and favouritism, without the post being properly advertised, without a written job description and person specification, without a formal application in writing, and without a formal interview. This kind of casual and outrageous favouritism is still not yet a thing of the past; more common nowadays, however, but just as serious, is the covert patronage behind many appointments to acting positions or to special projects or responsibilities. Second, there is the composition of the selection panel for the post of deputy head. However expert the interviewers, and however unbiased they are, it is difficult for justice to be seen to be done if they are all Exes; for if nothing else a selection panel consisting only of Exes will almost certainly be experienced differently by Exe candidates and Wye candidates, wih Exe candidates feeling supported but Wye candidates suspecting that there may be a basic lack of empathy and understanding for them. Third, there is the recurring emphasis in the story on 'performance', and on the ways in which the Exe teacher is subliminally groomed and coached, through the staffroom culture, to perform according to the expected norms. Performance is not the same as competence, however, and is an uncertain guide to competence.

Fourth, there is the point made right at the end of the story — most pupils, and at least half of the staff, are Wyes, though it is mainly Exes who get promotion to headships. In addition to the injustice to Wye teachers, there is the damage being done to Wye pupils, who do not have role models to imitate, nor friends at court in senior management, nor senior teachers to turn to for counselling and moral support. Fifth, there is the point being made through the use of algebraic symbols, X and Y : that all forms of unfair discrimination in appointments procedures operate in much the same way, regardless of whether the specific issues are to do with 'race', or with gender, or class, or disability. Sixth, and following on from this point, the story invites us to consider in depth and in detail how discrimination operates throughout the education system, and indeed throughout society, and to note that it's not just to do with attitudes but also with all sorts of customary and taken-for-granted (non-strange, so to speak) procedures and practices. Let us coin the term 'letterism' to summarise inequality between Exe people and Wye people, and describe letterism's separate features in turn.

But first, an emphasis on what letterism is not: it is not merely a set of beliefs inside people's heads, and it is not merely the programme of fascist organisations. In her reportage about Bradford and Birmingham in the late 1980s, Dervla Murphy gives many chilling accounts of the hostile and obscene views on 'race' matters which she came across amongst white people. She defines a racialist (sic) as 'someone to whom human beings are less worthy of respect and consideration if they belong to another race.'[2] As an implied definition of racialism this is adequate: but it will not do as an implied definition of racism. The latter refers not only to beliefs but also to behaviours, and to structures and patterns of organisation. The latter also emphasises that there is no objective factual basis by which humankind can be divided into 'races': 'races' themselves do not exist, even though certainly racism does; and though racism amongst other things does include the belief that there are entities and categories in the world which may be named as 'races'.

These points are extremely obvious to the vast majority of people who have given sustained thought to the matter, and it may seem wholly unnecessary to emphasise them here. But it is about the very definition of the term racism that there has been a significant national debate in recent years. The New Right, supported by the tabloid press, has been bidding to obliterate the distinction between racialism and racism, and to insist only on the narrow definition of racialism. In all sorts of ways, the New Right and the press have been successful in terms of the general climate of opinion and understanding in the country: they have found ready or even enthusiastic endorsement of their twisted package of proposals (a) that racialism doesn't actually exist; (b) that even it does there's nothing particularly wrong with it; and (c) that even if it is wrong it's so deep-rooted in human nature, and in Britain so much bound up with the splendours and glories of one of humankind's greatest historical achievements, viz the British Empire, that it would be wholly unrealistic and unreasonable to expect it to go away quickly. It is because of the popular success of these 'arguments' that letterism is described here.

Letterism is a dynamic process, not a state: a system of interacting sub-systems each drawing strength from, and each giving strength to, each of the others. Just as justice is both the ground and the consequence of equality, and just as equality is in its turn both the outcome of justice and its surest guarantee, so do the various sub-systems of letterism feed and sustain each other. There is vicious circle on vicious circle, knock-on effect on knock-on effect, downward spiral on downward vortex. (The metaphor of 'bricks in the wall' in this essay's title is inadequate to express the dynamic and interactive aspects of letterism: it does however evoke the sense that letterism is massive, and that it has many separate parts or components.)

At the heart of the system and process of letterism there is an interaction of three main types of factor, to do respectively with:

(i)   structures and relations of power;

(ii) beliefs and attitudes, and the cultural encounters and interchanges in which beliefs and attitudes are daily constructed and re-constructed;

(iii) procedures, behaviours, conventions, written and unwritten rules.[3]

Figure 2: Equality — three interacting factors

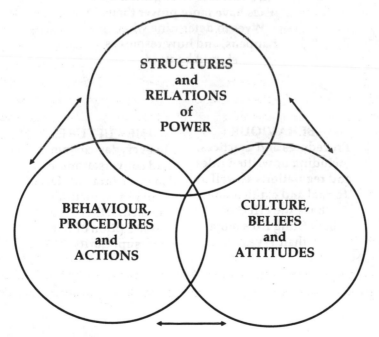

Each of these three sets of factors was glimpsed in the story of the two teachers. Thus (i) Exes more than Wyes were in the power-structure of the school, and were for example in the selection panels for senior posts. There was (ii) a belief in the staffroom culture that Exes 'perform' better than Wyes. And (iii) the procedures relating to appointments and promotions worked to the advantage of Exes more than Wyes. These three sets of factors overlap with each other, and also they stand in reciprocal, two-way causal relationships with each other. The overlaps can be shown visually in a Venn diagram, and the causal relationships in the same diagram with two-way arrows. (Figure 2)

To that initial diagram we can add immediately some brief notes about Exes and Wyes. (Figure 3)

The rest of this essay consists of a detailed unpacking of figure 3. Over 30 separable features of letterism will be noted. These are cogs and gear-whels in the machine, threads in the texture, weapons in the

Figure 3: Summary of Letterism

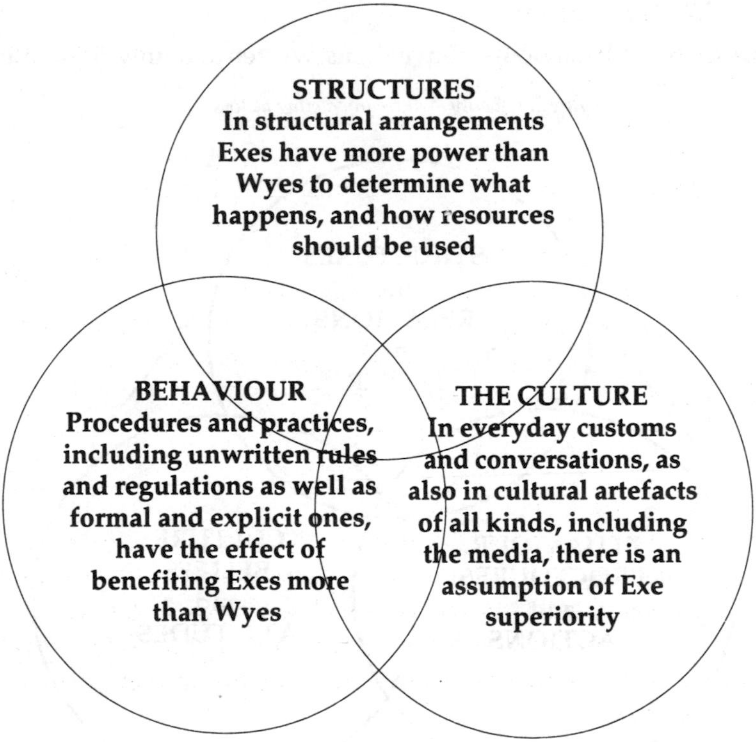

STRUCTURES
In structural arrangements
Exes have more power than
Wyes to determine what
happens, and how resources
should be used

BEHAVIOUR
Procedures and practices,
including unwritten rules
and regulations as well as
formal and explicit ones,
have the effect of
benefiting Exes more
than Wyes

THE CULTURE
In everyday customs
and conversations, as
also in cultural artefacts
of all kinds, including
the media, there is an
assumption of Exe
superiority

armoury, bricks in the wall. Each draws additional strength and vicious-ness from each of the others, and each is pernicious not only in itself but also in its contribution to the total package. The inventory has three main sections, corresponding to the three circles in figure 3. We start by considering structures and relations of power.

The Structures and relations of power

1) *At the top*

In the power structures of society, Exes are everywhere dominant — they are on the front benches in the House of Commons; the bishops' benches in the House of Lords; the benches of all kinds in the law courts; the saluting-boxes of parade-grounds; the top tables at ban-quets; the boards of directors or governors of both public and private enterprises; the flagships of the media; the platforms of school speech-days. Wyes, in contrast, are spectacularly absent from all such places.

2) *Who gets what*

Wherever Exes and Wyes are together it is Exes who take the lead, the chair, the limelight, the initiative, the honours, the lion's share.

3) *Religion*

In a letterist society it is Exes who supervise and control all religious worship and rites of passage, who define all creeds and orthodoxy, and who mediate all God's judgements on matters of public and personal morality.

4) *Violence and abuse.*

Wyes are far more likely than Exes to be physically or verbally attacked by other people, and many are a prey therefore to constant fear. Since all law and order agencies are controlled by Exes, the general trend is for violence against Exes to be treated by the courts far more severely than violence against Wyes.

5) *Goods*

As a consequence of having more power than Wyes, Exes have also more personal freedom and space, more health and well-being, and more opportunities for self-fulfilment through creative labour and leisure of various kinds. Exes, in short, have an undue share of society's goods.

6) *Bads*

Wyes, in contrast, have an undue share of bads (bad health, bad housing, bad and unfulfilling jobs, and forced custody and unfreedom of various kinds).

7) *No change*

The statistics about these various differentials are readily available, even in official documents published by the government, and these show that there has been relatively little change in inequalities over the years.

8) *Justice*

The overall arrangement cannot be justified as being in the interests of Wyes. Therefore, the inequality is unjust.

Beliefs and Attitudes

9) *Overlap*

There is an overlap, in a letterist system, between beliefs and attitudes on the one hand and structures and relations of power on the other.

10) *The media*

For beliefs and attitudes are formed, are constantly maintained on a day-to-day basis, through cultural artefacts — for example, and in particular, through the press and television — and it is Exes, not Wyes, who actually own or control the mass media, and who determine to what the media should attend and should not attend.[4]

11) *Conversations*

Beliefs and attitudes in any society and sustained not only by the mass media but also in countless day-to-day conversations and meetings, formal and informal — but in a letterist society there is both spatial and social distance between Exes and Wyes such that they very seldom meet each other in circumstances which permit or encourage them to engage in a shared enterprise of world-making.[5]

12) *Language*
A further difficulty in this respect is that interaction is expected always to be in Exe language — that is, the public, formal language of the society — not Wye language, which is looked down on usually as a mere dialect.

13) *Views of Wyes*
The stereotypical view of Wyes held by Exes is that they are unreliable, lazy, emotional, and not very intelligent or thoughtful. They may have a certain exotic charm, but are basically not capable of doing anything really important or serious.

14) *Exceptions*
Individual exceptions to this rule do exist, though, thus proving that the overall social system is fair, and that merit is recognised and rewarded if and when it exists.

15) *Views of Exes*
Exes see themselves, in contrast, as rational, intelligent, hard-working, energetic, and totally reliable.

16) *Dualisms*
In all manner of subtle and subliminal ways (as well as, in the most shameless of systems, in entirely unsubtle ways), Exe/Wye differences are seen to be analogous to 'natural' dichotomies such as light/dark, good/evil, god/devil, human/animal, reason/emotion, adult/child. Dualistic thinking is presumably not actually generated by Exe/Wye differences, but certainly it is enormously valuable for maintaining and strengthening them in the culture of everyday life.[6]

17) *Omission*
Such attitudes and beliefs are expressed entirely directly, but also often indirectly, through omission and silence.

18) *Internalising*
Alas, negative views of Wyes are often internalised by Wyes themselves. When this happens a crucial part of their education, in any process to change the overall letterist system, is unlearning — a

71

systematic critique and rejection of negative views taught to them over the years (or, indeed, over the centuries) by Exes.

19) *Anti-letterism*

The press and media not only present negative views of Wyes but also caricature and ridicule any attempts anywhere to address and challenge letterism, and to create letter equality. According to a much re-cycled fabrication in the tabloid press, for example, there is a London borough which has outlawed the use of the word 'because', on the grounds that it implies the prior use of the word 'why?' in such a way as to make Wyes sound subservient. Another borough, according to the tabloid press, has outlawed the use of the prefix 'ex' meaning 'former', since this could imply that letterism is no longer endemic throughout society; and has ruled also that no word beginning with 'ex' may be used if there are connotations of Exe superiority — eg words such as executive, executor and examiner. Self-styled satirists entertain themselves by inventing ALL (the Anti-Letterist League, whose supporters can be counted on the fingers of one hand, and officials on the thumbs of two); LETHAL (Lecturers Examiners Teachers and Headteachers Against Letterism, more deadly in its operations than in its aim); ALGAE (Anti-Letterist Guidelines and Exhortations, spawned all over the place); and CLEAN (Commission for Letter Equality and Niceness, a bunch of interfering prigs).

20) *Textbooks*

Amongst the cultural artefacts expressing and communicating messages of Exe superiority are the textbooks, syllabuses and programmes of study in schools. These overlap with, give strength to and are strengthened by, all the conventions, procedures, practices and rules of schools, for example those mentioned below.

Procedures and behaviours in schools

21) *Successes*

In schools the day-to-day procedures and conventions systematically benefit Exes, and work to the disadvantage of Wyes. Exes are in the highest sets, streams and classes, and in due course are far more likely to leave school with powerful examination successes, and to go on to higher education and highly-paid jobs.[7]

22) *Failures*

Wyes, in contrast, are in the lowest sets and streams, and receive an undue proportion of 'bads' — punishments, sanctions, rebukes and reprimands, suspensions, exclusions.

23) *Attention*

In day-to-day classroom interaction between teachers and pupils, Exe pupils receive a constant flow of attention, praise, affirmation and encouragement while Wyes learn daily to doubt their own ability and strength.

24) *Counter-culture*

In consequence Wye pupils frequently create their own Wye-friendly counter-culture, in which it is unpopular to strive for academic success — the done thing is to challenge and defy authority.

25) *Parents*

Exe parents come to school much more readily than Wye parents, and interact much more comfortably with teachers. Wye parents, on the contrary, are rather fearful and uneasy when they come into schools to meet teachers, and do not feel that they are being treated as adults, or as human beings with a genuine concern for the interests of children and young people.

26) *Expectations*

Schools' formal statements of aims always say grandly that they are concerned to help *all* children achieve their potential, 'irrespective' of whether they are Exes or Wyes. This sounds at first hearing a fine aspiration, and headteachers and governors never tire of announcing it. However, it is predicated on the assumption that the potential of Exe pupils is considerably greater than that of Wyes:

> *The Exe monarchs in their castle,*
> *The Wye peasants at their gate:*
> *All have their own potential,*
> *Ordained by their estate.*

27) *Denial of letterism*

And what their estate in life has ordained, schools, teachers and curricula daily reflect and confirm. There is seldom any open acknow-

LETTERISM IN SOCIETY AND EDUCATION

Circles and Spirals of Inequality between Exes and Wyes

Exes have superior
material conditions of life:
— wealth and capital
— freedom and choice
— health and lifespan
— working conditions
— housing

Wyes have mainly lowly
positions, and are unable to
affect events: they are
over-represented in:
— menial and poorly paid work
— unemployment
— underemployment
— custody of various kinds

Exes control the means of
communication, including in
particular the press and TV, and
have greater facility with public
(viz. 'standard') forms and
conventions of language

There is distance, both
spatial/physical and
social/ cultural between
Exes and Wyes

Wyes are by and large
invisible in the mass media,
and in other cultural artefacts
of mainstream society

Exes believe that Exes are
competent, intelligent, rational,
talented, active, industrious, etc,
and that Wyes on the contrary are
idle, feckless, emotional,
inefficient, and unreliable; such
beliefs may be internalised by
Wyes

Exes are dominant in:
— government and politics
— officialdom
— senior management
— law and order agencies
— education

STRUCTURES
in structural
arrangements Exes have
more power than Wyes to
determine what happens,
and how resources
should be used

THE CULTURE
In everyday customs
and conversations, as
also in cultural
artefacts of all kinds,
including the media,
there is an assumption
of Exe superiority

BEHAVIOUR
Procedures and practices,
including unwritten rules
and regulations as well as
formal and explicit ones,
have the effect of
benefitting Exes more

Textbooks and other
learning materials in
schools tend to reflect
cultural beliefs about Exe
superiority

Curriculum materials reflect Exe
experience of life, not Wye
experience, and are therefore less
accessible to Wyes than Exes

Syllabuses, schemes of work,
curriculum materials and teachers'
discourse do not acknowledge, let alone
affirm, Wyes' experience of letterism,
and do not help develop understanding

Exes succeed at school far more than
Wyes, and many Wyes become
disaffected

Most teachers in schools,
particularly in senior positions in
secondary schools are Exes

Recruitment and promotion
practices and procedures
lead to appointment of Exes
to senior positions

Wye pupils do not have role
models amongst the senior
staff, and do not have Wye
staff to counsel them

Wyes tend to be in lower sets and
classes, and to be learning less
academic subjects

Teachers have higher
expectations of Exe pupils than
of Wye, and give them more
encouragement

Exe parents receive a warmer
welcome than Wye when they
visit scools, and generally
have more in common with
the staff

ledgement, whether in formal syllabuses and 'attainment targets' or in casual day-to-day discussion and conversations amongst teachers and pupils, that letterism exists. Wye pupils' experience of letterism is thus not perceived as real, nor is the experience of their parents, families and communities. They are seldom or never encouraged to tell their own stories as Wye human beings, or to dream and shape distinctive Wye dreams.

28) *History*

Historic struggles against letterism in the past are similarly by and large not talked about or mentioned in textbooks, except when they can be shown as reflecting rather well on Exes. (For example, a number of history syllabuses do mention the benevolent work of certain Exe philanthropists in the nineteenth century.)

29) *Management*

There are relatively few Wye teachers in senior positions, for recruitment and selection procedures consistently operate to the benefit of Exes, to the point that many Wye teachers do not have confidence in their own abilities and do not venture to apply seriously and persistently for promotion.

30) *No models*

One consequence of this is that Wye pupils do not have powerful role models for themselves amongst the senior staff, nor do younger Wye teachers.

31) *No support*

Another consequence is that Wye pupils do not have ready access to supportive counselling from members of staff who understand them; further, they do not have powerful friends at court, so to speak — that is, teachers in the school's senior management team to speak and argue on their behalf.

The overall letterist system is shown in the chart on a separate page. The chart points out various interactions and influences, and emphasises in all its details how each aspect of the system is reinforced by, and in its turn gives reinforcement to, lots of other aspects.

The total picture is at first sight perhaps depressing, but it is also surely helpful. The principal benefit from seeing the picture as a whole is that it demonstrates that any serious attempt to dismantle letterism must be multi-dimensional — it is a package of co-ordinated and complementary measures which is required, not a one-off remedy or fix. This reminder is for most of us heartening rather than dispiriting. It goes hand in hand with an awareness that everyone needs allies, and that everyone, wherever they are and whoever they happen to be, has a significant role to play.

Finally, so what? What benefits may there be in this description and analysis of letterism? Would it not have been more helpful to give an account of racism, or sexism, or classism, or whatever? There are four main replies to this:

First, the term letterism surely stands a much better chance than more familiar terms of getting past the censoring devices and filters which most of us erect against any concept which we find at all threatening — and for various reasons, some of them more obvious and less creditable than others, terms such as racism and sexism, and anti-racism and anti-sexism, etc, have indeed become threatening in recent years, not least through the machinations and disinformation of the tabloid press. Second, the concept of letterism helps us to go beyond sloganising — it tries to unpack and unravel, reasonably patiently and without recriminations and resentment, how oppressive systems work in practice. Third, it emphasises the similarities between various kinds of oppression in terms of their internal dynamics, and in terms therefore of the practical strategies which are required to change and replace them.

Fourth, it stands a chance of evoking from everyone, including those who in real life are Exes, a certain sympathy and empathy for Wyes. Such sympathy and empathy are not sufficient as motivating forces in the overall change process, but they are essential. All Exes have, somewhere in their past and in their psyche, experiences of having been a Wye. They need to be in contact with those experiences if, in the total struggle against letterism, they are to play their parts with courage and commitment, and with craft and skill. And with deep and due awareness that an anti-letterist who is nothing but an anti-letterist is not really an anti-letterist.

7. Manifesto for Inequality
— some features of the new era

The 1990s in British education are the decade of the Education 'Reform' Act. Similarly in many other countries there is currently a regression , directed and managed by the central government, from certain inspirational ideals of the past — in particular those concerned with learner-centred education, and with education for equality. At the same time that we try to resist the so-called reforms, we have to acknowledge that certainly there has been much wrong with education, and that it is 'transformation' which is required rather than 'reform'.

This piece was written in autumn 1987, at the time of the national consultation about, as it then was, the Reform Bill. It is a piece of passionate polemic, and for this reason does not acknowledge that the new legislation opens up valuable new opportunities at the same time that it threatens and restricts. This is admittedly a weakness, in the overall context of this book. The piece is reprinted here, however, as a reminder of some important aspects of the national climate at the present time, and therefore of the background against which education for equality and learner-centred education have to make, if they do, their way.

* * * * *

PREAMBLE

1. We hold this truth to be self-evident, that human beings are created unequal.

2. There is amongst us inequality of talent, intelligence and virtue; of capacity to enjoy freedom and create wealth; and of ability to rule, lead, organise and contribute to an ordered, harmonious and decent society.

3. Grave threats are posed to our civilisation by those who preach the pernicious gospel that inequality is neither right nor inevitable. They include not only atheistic and communistic states on the international scene but also certain people within our own society. Their ideas gain plausibility amongst the idle, the envious and the unlettered. They must be vigorously suppressed.

4. The country's education system has a vital role to play in hallowing, protecting and furthering inequality. We therefore propose the ten-point plan which follows. Its goal is to return the British education system to its historic and essential task, which is that of preparing the young to take up their rightful places in society as either leaders or led, and to accept, appreciate and *enjoy* inequality.

TEN-POINT PLAN FOR EDUCATIONAL REFORM

1. **Curriculum**
   We will ensure that all schools teach the same basic nationalistic curriculum. It will consist of ten subjects, to act as foundation stones for the society which we wish to build and maintain. The subjects must be kept meticulously separate from, and totally uncontaminated by, each other. The term 'nationalistic' may on occasions be shortened to 'national'.

2. **Testing**
   We will ensure that all children regularly have their memory tested, at the ages of 7, 11, 14, and 16, in each of the foundation subjects. The results of the tests will be published, so that inequalities of talent and memorising ability are entirely plain, and so that from the earliest stages children are groomed, according to their different needs, for competition, success, pride and failure.

3. **Local control**

   We will ensure that each school is controlled by a board of governors. This board will supervise the local introduction of the nationalistic curriculum, and the local publication of test results. Its members will be drawn from groups sympathetic to the ideals and principles of inequality: in particular from the senior management of large-scale industry and commerce but also, of course, from local police forces.

4. **A note on terminology**

   We recognise that the term 'local controllers' may not have the friendly image which we wish to project. Accordingly we propose that the local controllers and supervisors of schools should normally be referred to as 'parents'.

5. **Controversy**

   We will ensure that, so far as possible, teachers avoid teaching about controversial subjects. Most of the time the new nationalistic curriculum will itself prevent controversy arising. But certain teachers may lack the competence and expertise to avoid controversy completely. Such teachers will be expected to follow carefully the following guidelines:

   (i)   *Sex:* The proper place for women is the home, and the education of girls must always bear this in mind. Sexual behaviour, other than within marriage, is usually immoral, frequently deviant, and invariably regrettable.

   (ii) *Religion:* Christianity is clearly superior to all other religions, or so-called religions.

   (iii) *Politics:* There is no place in schools for extremist political views, for example views which question the principles in this manifesto.

6. **Culture**

   We will ensure that British values are paramount. The curriculum and ethos of our schools, the textbooks that are used, the displays, everything must reflect and sustain pride in our nation and things British. This must be made very clear to immigrants. The term 'education for racial equality' is highly inflammatory and unpatriotic and implies an aggressive campaign designed to brainwash people; it must not be used. Equally unacceptable are terms such as 'multicultural', 'education for international understanding', 'world studies' and 'bilingual'.

7. **Influence**

Our only remotely significant opponents are certain locally-elected politicians, aided and abetted by various unrepresentative members of the teaching force, and by a number of misguided education officers and politicised advisers. We will ensure that their influence is severely curtailed and, if possible, removed.

We intend a package of measures to achieve this, including delegation of financial decisions and appointment of teaching staff to local controllers (known as 'parents' — item 4 above), and central government sponsorship and financial assistance for individual schools which have been particularly successful at promoting inequality. This latter measure will be known as 'opting out'. The new schools thus created will be permitted, indeed expected, to limit entry only to those children whose parents accept the ideals in this manifesto.

8. **Ladders to success**

We will ensure that a number of carefully selected children from poor homes, including perhaps even some children or grandchildren of immigrants, are allowed to succeed at school, and to go to university. This will demonstrate to everyone that our educational system is fair and just, and will help generate gratitude, loyalty and affection.

9. **The arts and imagination**

We will ensure that access to literature, religion and the creative arts is limited to those few children who are capable of appreciating them, and whose parents can afford to pay the extra costs involved, and will guard vigorously against the danger of allowing immature minds to 'express' themselves or to be 'imaginative', 'playful', 'satirical' or 'prophetic'.

10. **Complementary measures**

We will ensure that our educational reforms are strengthened by other legislation which we are introducing to increase inequality — in particular, our measures to reduce public expenditure on health, housing and welfare benefits; to curb the powers of trade unions; to introduce a poll tax; and to curb immigration by re-defining the concept of British nationality. Insofar as our educational reforms are not immediately successful we shall be happy, indeed keen, to introduce the following:

(i) Compulsory military service, to complete the education of those who fail at school.

(ii) Reduced taxes on alcohol, tranquillisers and burglar alarms.

(iii) Special Arts Council grants and subsidies for the makers of TV soap operas.

(iv) A much enlarged police-force.

(v) Humane psychiatric treatment for members of the teaching force who are unable to cope.

CONSULTATION

This draft manifesto has been issued for public consultation. However, the closing-date for the receipt of your comments has unfortunately passed.

8. Accustomed As We Are
— an ethnographic footnote

May she dwell,wishes Yeats in his Prayer for My Daughter, in 'a house/ Where all's accustomed, ceremonious'. For 'how but in custom and in ceremony are innocence and beauty born?' A problem is that the opposites of innocence and beauty (which for Yeats in that poem are respectively hatred and arrogance) are also given birth by custom and ceremony. Negatives are nursed and nourished by the routines and rituals of everyday culture just as much as positives. Consider, for example, an office-party as a cultural event: fearful, oppressive, cynical and destructive aspects of organisational culture may be readily glimpsed there if such qualities are present also in the organisation's structures and procedures.

This piece has its roots in some real events. It was written in order to express sympathy and solidarity towards one particular person who had been unwarrantably hurt, and in order to explore and ponder, for colleagues likely to be interested, the concept of organisational culture. The events to which the piece was responding had been on the surface frothy and light-hearted: the response to them had to avoid being stuffy or solemn, yet also had to be in some way serious. Combating racism, and all that, includes sometimes — does it? — penning pieces such as this.

* * * * *

Dear Brian

I'm writing to congratulate you on your farewell speech at the office party last week. Very funny and with pinprick accuracy, just the sort of thing we all needed. These rituals are usually an awful chore and a bore, but you breathed new life into the one last week. At best there's a real community spirit in our office, almost a family feeling, and parties are a time for bringing it alive.

You were lucky, I suppose, to have that joke about funerals handed to you on a plate. Who could have guessed that Bob would have a family bereavement last week, and that you'd be able to make those hilarious — if, Brian, *slightly* macabre — remarks. It's always a nuisance when someone is away from the office for a family funeral, not just because of the work left undone but because it encourages unhealthy thoughts about transience, and all that. Don't let anyone tell you that your remarks were in bad taste — they were exquisite, Brian, exquisite.

Was it luck or was it cleverness that enabled you to get hold of old Paul's confidential self-appraisal papers? They were deplorably analytical and navel-gazing, and also of course uncharacteristically frank and self-aware, and you were quite right to read out the juiciest bits. The office would be sheer chaos if people let it all hang out all over the place and then thought they could hide behind a mask of confidentiality. Old Paul himself wasn't exactly chuffed, as you can guess, but everyone else thought that this part of your speech was absolutely necessary as well as gorgeously funny.

We also appreciated the way you put your secretary in her place. She makes a delightful sacrificial victim, I must say, and I'm sure all the other girls got the point.

Which reminds me of your lesbianism joke. Splendid, Brian, splendid. You tactfully reminded all the female staff what their role in life is, but at the same time made it absolutely clear that the chaps aren't really all that interested in them, and certainly couldn't care less if they sometimes seem to be resistant to our charms. Your remark was timely and masterly as well as typically subtle. Ignore the feminist backlash. It'll soon die down.

And then your handicapped people joke, the single parent family joke, the people round the office getting decrepit joke, your Geoffrey Boycott story, the judiciously chosen profanities, all tremendously good. The climax for me, and I think for everyone else as well, but particularly those of us in more responsible positions, was your crack about equal opportunities policies.

Everyone in the office knows, and everyone knows that everyone in the office knows, but no one in the office dares blurt out, that equal opportunities policies are a disaster area, the silliest thing since the Sermon on the Mount. It was refreshing and invigorating to have them ridiculed so unambiguously by yourself, particularly — this was lovely — since it was you who chaired the committee which drafted our loony policy in the first place.

You mustn't let yourself be worried by criticisms from some of our bleeding heart colleagues, the types who like to look at the *Guardian* after a day's work in the real world. What you said needed saying. It was an inspired touch, may I add, to imply that you have no confidence in the ability of our new colleague whose job is to steer the office's equality policies on race. Your remark about her was 100% libellous, of course, no doubt about it, but no-one will dare object, you did it so delicately.

All in all what I appreciate is that you played the game, you didn't let the side down. Making speeches at office parties is one of the rituals which we senior people have to go through from time to time. Somehow we have to remind the other ranks what and where ultimate reality is, and yet also to let them think they can take one or two slight liberties, can transgress on occasions over certain lines. It's terribly difficult to get it right — to hit the right balls to the right boundaries, as Levi-Strauss or Durkheim probably said, I shouldn't be surprised.

But nice one, Brian you were really elegant. All good wishes at the threshold of your new job, you'll go places, I'm sure.

References
(1) 'The symbolic function of ritual is to relate the individual through ritualistic acts to a social order, to heighten respect for that order, to revivify that order within the individual and, in particular, to deepen acceptance of the procedures used to maintain continuity,

order and boundary and which control ambivalence towards the social order.'
— from *Ritual in Education,* by Basil Bernstein, H.L. Elvin and R.S. Peters, in Philosophical Transactions of the Royal Society of London B (1966), 251(772), 429-36.

(2) 'Any man's death diminishes me...therefore never send to know for whom the bell tolls.'
— from *Devotions,* by John Donne, 1571-1631.

9. Fragments and Fancies
— the case of Elephant Education

The 'devouring' tendency in humankind, said Blake in The Marriage of Heaven and Hell, is fearful of the senses, of creativity, of energy, of delight, and 'takes portions of existence and fancies that the whole.' Also naive and destructive is the supposition that wholes are ever built or grasped by adding up fragments. The structuring of human knowledge into school subjects for example, most notoriously at present, into the 'foundation' subjects of the national curriculum in Britain — involves the very kind of mindless and heartless splitting which Blake deplored. One solution, we too readily suppose, is to emphasise the importance of so-called 'cross-curricular concerns'. But they too can be as isolating, fragmenting and partial as timetabled subjects.

'Elephant Education', based on a famous Indian folktale, names and poses the problem, and recalls a couple of big words, integrity and love, as values to start from and return to. Alas, however, the fable has no answers or practical programme. But maybe, sometimes, the playful posing of problems has a certain value in its own right?

* * * * *

'The world we live in,' said the official report, 'contains elephants. The country's education system should therefore reflect our need to know about and to understand elephants. Policies should be developed, and resources provided, for more and better quality elephant education.'

'Elephant education!' exclaimed the people when they heard this recommendation. 'We are not entirely sure what that is.' Six blind people went forth to find out.

The first blind person went to the Ivory Coast in West Africa, since this is a country actually named after elephants, albeit only partially. This first blind person studied the records and the record of the *Parti Democratique de la Cote d'Ivoire,* its struggle for independence, its life in and out of the French Community, its affairs with de Gaulle, its use of power, pressure and resources over forty years; and concluded that elephant education is basically another term for political education.

The second blind person went to a film called The Elephant Man, and studied elephantiasis, the swelling of limbs, the development of obstructions in the flow of lymph and the overgrowth of subcutaneous tissue; and in looking thus at sickly growth and wrong progress, and comparing it with healthy growth and right progress, this second blind person concluded that elephant education is basically another term for development education.

The third blind person studied the diverse ways in which human beings relate to elephants. We corral them in keddahs, hump them with howdahs, train them for traction, process them in parades, zombify them in zoos, surround them in circuses. This third blind person saw not only diversity but bars and barriers, exploitation, prejudice and discrimination, constraints on freedom; and concluded that elephant education is basically another term for multicultural anti-racist education.

The fourth blind person studied the escalation in the arms race which took place when Hannibal of Carthage, in 220 BC, resolved to use elephants in his war of liberation against the particular form of imperialism known as *pax romana.* Seeing thus both direct and structural violence this fourth blind person concluded that elephant education is basically another term for peace education.

91

The fifth blind person went to an American-style fast-food restaurant, and studied on its menu the array of Jumbo burgers, Jumbo sandwiches and Jumbo pizzas; reading between as well as along the lines of the menu, the fifth blind person had a vision of prairies and boardrooms, and of men doing there what men have to do; and recalled that behind every good man there is *Kirche und Küche*, temple and table, synagogue and sink, shrine and shine, mosque and mop, church and chore. This fifth blind person concluded that elephant education is another term for equal opportunities and anti-sexist education.

The sixth blind person studied a distinctive literary genre in which the inner and essential nature of elephants is frequently explored and expressed. It consists of a litany of interrogatives and responses. Interrogative, why do elephants paint the soles of their feet yellow? — Response, so that they can float upside down in the custard without being seen. Interrogative, how can you tell when you are in bed with an elephant? — Response, because he has an E embroidered on his pyjama jacket. Studying this literary genre the sixth blind person realised that elephants must suffer from a negative self-image and, very probably, from a lack of adequate assertiveness training, and concluded that elephant education is another term for personal and social education.

The six blind people went their separate ways, and polished separately their respective conclusions. They applied separately for money from charitable trusts and from local and central government; set up separate working-parties, networks, professional associations, standing conferences, committees of enquiry; published separate journals, magazines, bulletins and newsletters; set up separate resource centres and support services; formulated separate sets of aims, objectives and schemes of work, and separately approached examination boards to provide accreditation for them; competed for the attention of headteachers, and for space, time, resources and energy in each and every individual school in the land.

They completely failed, however, to realise any of the values which they wished to promote; and failed also to avert any of the threats to which they wished to respond. They failed even to live out the short span of their own lives with integrity and with love.

PART THREE:
THE TEACHER AND THE LEARNER

10. How Learners Learn
— a mnemonic for most seasons

This is a continuation, so to speak, of the earlier essay entitled Learning towards Justice. *That earlier essay distinguished between four main kinds of stance towards prevailing power-structures, and argued that a choice is required for 'transforming' stances as distinct from 'conforming' ones, whilst at the same time avoiding the Scylla of 'reforming' and the Charybdis of 'deforming'.*

Such a choice is demanded of teachers in relation to the power structures of the education system as well as to those of wider society. Therefore a major purpose of all inservice training programmes and staff development activities should be to enable this choice to be clarified and made. Teachers in their turn should be helping their pupils in such choosing.

Yes, but how? What would an individual inservice day ('Baker Day') look like, and what would be the distinctive features of an individual classroom lesson, if these were the underlying concerns? And what would a course of study or training as a whole look like — what would be its overall structure, its pattern, its rhythm?

These are the questions addressed in this essay. The essay is intended to be relevant both for the planning of inservice training, including one-off inservice days, and for the design of courses and modules in schools. It draws on much the same body of theory as was used in the essay entitled

Learning towards Justice — *that is, the theory of conscientisation developed by Paulo Freire and his co-workers — and suggests a simple and user-friendly memorising device by which the theory can be called readily and accessibly to mind.*

* * * * *

I wish', says a child in a poem by James Berry, daydreaming at the back of the classroom:

> *'I wish my teacher's eyes wouldn't*
> *go past me today. I wish he'd know*
> *know it's okay to hug me when I kick*
> *a goal. Wish I myself wouldn't*
> *hold back when an answer comes.'*

It is a beautiful statement of what every learner requires first and foremost: to be noticed, to be attended to, to be valued, to be affirmed. Out of that attention and affirmation grow the confidence and, yes, the courage to learn: if the teacher dares to teach, that is, to attend to and care for the learners, then the learners in their turn can dare to learn.

It is an axiom of sound inservice education that teachers should be taught in the same way that they, in their turn, ought to teach others. And it is an axiom of sound classroom teaching that children and young people are not intrinsically different from adults so far as learning is concerned, and that the insights and practical procedures of adult education are therefore as relevant and valuable in school classrooms as they are at inservice courses. However, these twin axioms are all too often honoured in the breach rather than the observance.

We are anxious, certainly, to avoid both frying pan and fire, both devil and deep blue sea. For example, we are anxious to avoid providing talks and lectures which are merely boring and uninvolving, and which merely seem to communicate messages about the superior knowledge of the speaker. (The archetypal bad lecture, nowadays, involves an overhead transparency with most of it masked out. The lecturer then slowly draws the mask down the 'page', providing usually not the dawning revelations which are presumably intended but a dramatisation of that old playground chant : 'I know something you don't know'.)

And also, we wish to avoid providing aimless 'discussions' . Trouble is, we all too often provide the worst of both worlds : lectures, talks, overhead transparencies and presentations which fail to connect with issues which are currently of most concern to the learners, and which therefore convey a message of not valuing their experience and perceptions; interspersed with waffly, point-scoring group discussions in which the most confident persons present (confident by virtue of their personality, seniority or articulacy rather than because of their relevant knowledge and experience) repeat unreflectingly things which they have said umpteen times before in other places, and in which others feel increasingly alienated and angry, or demoralised and depressed.

Yet our aspirations are basically right. Courses of study do need to include the collective examination of perspectives and overviews, and the authoritative presentation of experience, and of reflection-on-experience, which good lectures characteristically provide. Equally they need participation: opportunities for each person present to question and clarify, to think aloud, to listen to and learn from others, to share — yes,to share, not just chat about — his or her personal experience and perceptions, and in these ways to modify and to extend their understanding.

One solution which is sometimes used, to avoid the disadvantages both of lectures and of discussions, and yet to embody their respective benefits, is a 'structured discussion activity' or, in a simpler and more modest phrase, a 'discussion exercise'. Such exercises are useful both in school classrooms with pupils and on inservice courses with their teachers. There is an extended description of discussion exercises, and of their features and potential practical advantages, in the chapter in this book entitled *Talking as Equals: the moral culture of the classroom*. The purpose of this essay is to consider the overall framework in which discussion exercises have a distinctive place and role, and their relationship both to chalk-and-talk and to genuine discussion and dialogue. The essay is concerned with pupils in schools and equally with their teachers in inservice training, since the same principles of learning are relevant for all.

Discussion exercises of many kinds have been described in various manuals and handbooks.[1] A single example will suffice here. It is of an exercise which is particularly useful very near to the start of a course or conference. Learners are given envelopes containing nine or so slips of paper. On each slip there is a quotation or statement — of at most 60 or 70 words in length — from a book or article relevant to the theme of the course. Working in pairs, learners rank these extracts in the order in which they would like to discuss them in greater detail, or in the order in which they agree with the emphases being made. Then in groups of four or six, they explain their various rank orders to each other. Third and finally, the group as a whole lists the main questions and issues which it would now like to consider further.[2]

Such an exercise has some of the advantages of a lecture: all learners are attending to the same body of external material, and this material comes to them from various authoritative sources. The activity also has the advantages of a genuine discussion: all learners contribute their ideas, all have a measure of control over sequence and pace, all question and clarify, all listen to others, all derive a certain satisfaction from being attended to seriously by others.

But such an exercise is neither a lecture nor a genuine discussion. This point must be acknowledged and emphasised. A structured activity such as this is an alternative to, and a preparation for, lectures and discussions: it is not, however, a substitute for them. A course or conference consisting only of discussion exercises would be merely frivolous and frustrating.

The task for the teacher or course organiser, then, is to construct a judicious mix of (a) exercises, (b) lectures and presentations, and (c) genuine discussion. The mix necessarily has to exist in a temporal sequence, and therefore a better term than mix would be pattern, or rhythm, or process. Inevitably the pattern has to be described sequentially, and therefore terms such as 'phase' or 'stage' are not inappropriate. However, helpful metaphors can also be drawn from music. The separate aspects of a course of study are not only like separate movements, one following after another, but are also like motifs, themes or tunes: there are reprises, revisitings and prefigurings as well as a time for each to be dominant, and each separate theme derives texture and colouring from each of the others.

When planning the mix of activities in a course of study, and arranging them into a sequence or pattern, you use a theory — a theory of how people learn. You need to able to have ready access to this theory when thinking on your feet, and this access needs to be not only to the theory as a whole but also, speedily and unfussily, to any one of its constituent parts. Therefore you perhaps need also a simple mnemonic — a memorising device which will enable you to call your theory easily to mind, or any one part of it, and to describe it accessibly and in a user-friendly way to others. This essay recalls the theories of learning which have been developed in adult education circles over the last 30 years or so, and argues that they are relevant not only for the planning and organisation of inservice courses for teachers but also for many courses of study in school classrooms, particularly courses in the humanities and social studies. The theories are evoked with terms such as 'experiential learning', 'action learning', and 'learning through reflection and action'.[3] They have in common that they do not make a sharp distinction between theoretical learning on the one hand and practical activity on the other, nor do they envisage some sort of linear relationship between theory and practice, with theory typically leading into practice. Further, and more importantly, the essay proposes a mnemonic or memorising device, the word A-G-E-N-D-A. The six letters of this word, it is proposed, can be made to refer conveniently to six main things which need to be done in any course of study, whether with pupils in classrooms or with their teachers on inservice courses, and to six main motifs or themes which need to be present. In summary, the mnemonic goes as follows:

A **acknowledging, accepting, affirming, aims and actuality for all**

G **getting to grips with the group's grievances and the gritty-nitty**

E **enquiring into the experiences, experiments, endeavours and enterprises of equals**

N **noting notions**

D **deliberating, debating, drafting, declaring, demonstrating**

A **agreeing on action, and acting**

This mnemonic seems sturdy but not rigid, memorable but not dictating, pliant but not slippery, user-friendly but not casual. It has the additional advantage that the word 'agenda' means originally simply 'things to be done' and yet has nicely both a literal and a metaphorical meaning: we speak of the agenda of a specific meeting but also, metaphorically, of such and such a matter being on, or not on, the political agenda, and so on.

Each of these six phases or motifs will be taken here in turn and explained in more detail. The theories of learning to be outlined here are drawn, to repeat, from adult education, not from the accidents of the English alphabet and the English lexicon: the purpose of turning to the latter is to provide something reasonably memorable, not — of course — to provide the theory itself.

A: acknowledging, accepting and affirming aims and actuality for all
All too many inservice courses and conferences for teachers start with what the organisers call a keynote address or major input. The trouble with such starts is that however inspirational and authoritative the lecturer the implicit message is that the audience consists only of empty vessels — only of people with no relevant or valuable experience of their own. Self-respect may be undermined rather than enhanced, and in any case much of what the lecturer says goes — in that old phrase — in at one ear and out at the other, because people have not yet had a chance to collect and deploy their own thoughts. You can only take in what somebody else has to tell you if first you have tidied and organised your mind to receive it. Lecturer and audience have to be on the same wave-length if there is to be communication, and such accord of frequencies is most unlikely to happen by accident.

Learners are helped to tune in if the experience and knowledge which they bring are acknowledged, and accepted and affirmed as basic and valid starting points. These three tasks — acknowledging, accepting, affirming — cannot be accomplished by a lecture, and are unlikely to be accomplished through a process of free discussion, particularly if people do not know each other or — the contrary difficulty — if they know each other so well that all their free discussions fall into pre-determined grooves. They can, however, be accomplished through a structured discussion activity.

As at inservice courses for teachers so also in the day-to-day classroom: start where the learners are, what they know already, what they care about, what they are interested in. Do not start with the syllabus, or with your own interests, or with the so-called attainment targets of the national curriculum; and do not — this is the immensely more important point — charge an admission price, which effectively means that some or all of the learners have to shed, together so to speak with their anoraks, precious parts of their identity and history before they can cross the threshold of your classroom. These precious parts of themselves include their culture, language and dialect, and countless experiences, stories and memories of their families, communities and friends, including in particular stories and experiences of oppression and injustice. Every

101

course of study must start with, and contain throughout, an affirmation of the actual for all.

G: Getting to grips with the group's grievances and with the gritty-nitty

The lexicon lets us down slightly on the letter G, for the word 'grievance' does not capture the whole concern, or any way not immediately or at first sight. However, if grievance means awareness of what is not right, and if right means both just and correct, then grievance is truly *le mot juste*. It is essential that learners should identify and analyse (a) objective realities which are unjustly working to their disadvantage and also (b) ideas, understandings and thoughts of their own which are inconsistent with each other, and some of which must therefore be in some important sense incorrect.

G sounds here, and is intended to sound, fairly uncomfortable and threatening and, therefore, inconsistent with the warm and accepting embrace of A. How can the two be reconciled? One approach, as commended and advocated by Paulo Freire and his co-workers, is to 'encode' the grievances into narratives or images of various kinds. These are learner-friendly and non-threatening in precisely the same way that the parables in the New Testament are learner-friendly and non-threatening — they make sense only to those who have ears to hear, and eyes to see. Such images and codifications may in the first instance be, quite literally, pictorial. Freire himself used line-drawings, but other workers, for example the Swedish educator Andreas Fuglesang, have preferred photographs. Either way the pictures should involve the 'imitative reproduction of reality', in Fuglesang's phrase, as distinct from the prettifying or caricaturing style of illustration used by many publishers of children's books and school textbooks in Western countries. 'When you live in reality', writes Fuglesang, 'sometimes you are not able to see it. The picture lifts the mind out of reality.'[4] The purpose of such lifting, he emphasises, is to 'trigger in the community a dialogue about its reality that will possibly lead to decisions and actions to alter that reality'. It is interesting and significant that the learner, for Fuglesang, is a collective — 'the community' — not, as in the vast majority of the world's classrooms, and as in the new national curriculum enshrined into the law of the land in Britain, an individual. This point is captured by the reference to groups — 'getting to grips with the group's grievances' — in our mnemonic.[5]

Codifications and images of grievances can of course be provided in other media besides pictures. Grievances can be dramatised in street-theatre or puppet plays, or in fables or metaphors, and can be presented also through what are sometimes called 'problem stories'.[6] Whatever the medium of codification, the process of decoding has four components or aspects, corresponding to the four main questions present in any and every problematique: (i) what is the problem here — that is, what is it that hurts, how do we name it? (ii) what do we understand to be the background causes of the problem in history and in human institutions? (iii) what should be done, both by ourselves and by others, and in both the short-term and the longer, to solve, manage or live with the problem? and (iv) what are our underlying values in all this, and what are the features of the better world or situation we are seeking to create?[7]

E : enquiring into, examining and evaluating endeavours, essays, experiences and experiments by equals

The lexicon is really bountiful for us here. The words it provides say so much that very little is required by way of further explanation. Suffice to say that the third phase of a course of study, coming immediately after a phase concerned with identifying and analysing problems, should be concerned with finding out what other people have done to solve or manage similar problems elsewhere. The terms endeavour, essay, experience, experiment emphasise that the enquiry should be through concrete case-studies, not through theoretical or idealised accounts. The term equal in the mnemonic ('..endeavours by *equals*') emphasises that the case-studies should be presented by, or minimally from the point of view of, people whose interests in the affair are similar to those of the learners themselves. At inservice courses for teachers, for example, case-studies should be presented by teachers; it follows, rather romantically and unrealistically, but surely stimulatingly, that a high proportion of the textbooks which we use in schools should be written by children.

N : noting notions

Again, as with G, the lexicon appears at first sight to let us down — it appears to provide us with niggardly and inadequate words. But again, as with G, further reflection reveals the riches of our dear language, not its meanness. The word 'notion' is closely synonymous with words such as theory, concept, conceptualisation, abstraction, idea: the N phase of a course is the phase in which there is an encounter, indeed confrontation, with theory. But 'notion' also has connotations of untrue, unproven, unpolished, unfinalised. It is therefore precisely the word we need: for all theories, in the natural sciences as well as in the social sciences, are provisional and unfinished. It is very important indeed that learners should be aware of this.

The word 'noting' in the mnemonic recalls a time-honoured activity in all educational institutions, that of giving and taking notes: time-honoured and also, all too often, time-wasting. It implies also taking note, however, as distinct from taking notes: and this, most certainly, is essential in all learning. Learners need at least to take note of, that is, to be aware of and to pay attention to, ideas, theories and concepts worked out by others. It is in the enquiry and notions phases of a course that lectures and presentations of various kinds are most appropriate and effective.

D : discussing, debating, disagreeing, deliberating, drafting, declaring, demonstrating

The lexicon again showers us with blessings here, to recall a whole series of inter-related matters which have to be seen to towards the end of a course. The first emphasis is on discussion and disagreement — real discussion now, as distinct from that which was occasioned by the structured activities earlier in the course. In the early 1970s a team of American educators devised what they called the 'We Agree Process' and the 'We Agree Workshop'.[8] It was a useful and important set of devices and procedures for getting a group of teachers — typically, the whole staff of a single school — to come to a consensus on such and such a matter, and then to make firm plans on the basis of this consensus. Such a process is sorely needed in many British school staffrooms in the 1990s as teachers battle and struggle through Baker Days. But whilst agreement and consensus are appropriate goals to strive for, they are not necessarily also the process and means to those goals. What teachers need in the first instance is not agreement but a strong institutional framework to contain, and indeed to facilitate, disagreements: we need, so to speak, a 'We Disagree Process', and a series of 'We Disagree Workshops'. Similarly the pupils in our classrooms need opportunities, provided and structured by the teacher, for handling dissonance, discord and disagreement. 'Without contraries there is no progression'.

But certainly disagreement is not a be-all-and-end-all. It should lead into activities of declaring and demonstrating, and these in their turn depend on activities of drafting. A declaration, in the present context, is a carefully thought-out statement of general principles, of abstractions, of crystallisations of theory. It reflects and represents wisdom after the event — the events, that is to say, of the earlier parts of the course. It expresses also wisdom before the event — before the next part of the course, which is to be about actual and practical action. Insofar as the declarations which are produced are written, as distinct from presented through some other medium (drama, video, visual display or exhibition etc) then most certainly they need to go through a series of separate drafts, and this drafting process should involve learners working collectively rather than as separate individuals. If the declaration is through some other medium then the term 'drafting' is less appropriate: but still there is most definitely a need for continual revision and review, rehearsal, trial and error, continual going back to the drawing board and starting again. The process is painful, for there is discarding and unlearning as well as building. A purpose of the structured discussion activities in the earlier part of the course was to provide the courage and persistence which such discarding and unlearning now require.

The term 'demonstrating' implies a declaration which is made public outside the boundaries of the course itself, and implies also some sort of ritual or symbolic action which signals that people are committed to their declaration of principles, and that they mean to defend them and to act on them.

A : agreeing on action, and acting

Just the right words again. The learners finally decide, in the light of the declaration of general principles debated and drafted in the previous phase of the course, what should be done in practice, and they do it. The English word acting has connotations of pretending, role-playing, maskadopting — and, indeed, the action which is taken may be symbolic rather than real in the first instance; instead or as well, it may be tentative and experimental, with inner commitment following, not preceding, external behaviour.

The glorious thing about the letter A, in the context of our mnemonic, is that it is both ending and beginning: it ends one agenda but begins another. This is shown visually in Figure 5. The learning process is

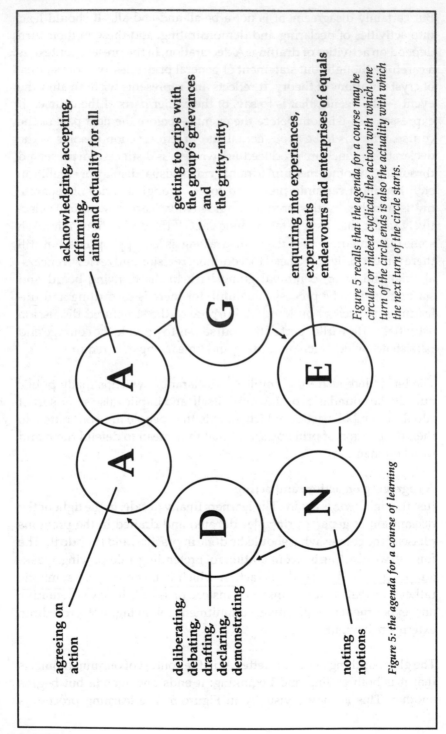

acknowledging, accepting, affirming, aims and actuality for all

getting to grips with the group's grievances and the gritty-nitty

enquiring into experiences, experiments endeavours and enterprises of equals

Figure 5 recalls that the agenda for a course may be circular or indeed cyclical: the action with which one turn of the circle ends is also the actuality with which the next turn of the circle starts.

agreeing on action

deliberating, debating, drafting, declaring, demonstrating

noting notions

Figure 5: the agenda for a course of learning

cyclical not linear, and the mnemonic nicely catches and emphasises this. Thus the action with which one cycle ends is also the actuality which at the beginning of the next cycle is acknowledged, accepted and affirmed. Learning is a continuous revolution.

At the heart of that revolution there is the learner seeking, and needing, attention and affirmation: now, this day, this minute. James Berry's child is the essential and inescapable reality, is what it's all about: 'I wish my teacher's eyes wouldn't go past me today.'

*****

APPENDIX — SOME PROBLEM STORIES

This set of problem stories derives from a workshop for teachers in Lesotho, Southern Africa[9]. Nobody outside Lesotho will understand all the acronyms and local references, but the essential underlying issues are very clear. The stories are reprinted here to explain and illustrate the concept of 'problem story' in detail, and as a reminder that the qualities of daring and perseverance required of teachers are much the same all over the world. There is further brief reference to the workshop in the introduction to the piece in this book entitled *Truths about Bias*.

'Manual work's a waste of time'
Our school started in January 1981. Development Studies was introduced in Form A instead of history and geography. Last term the Form B's were spending two hours a week on a very successful practical project on soil erosion. Hearing about this, Ntate Liphoto went to the school Manager, and said he wanted his son to do 'proper' subjects, so that he could go on to High School. 'The children shouldn't be wasting their time doing manual work', he said. The school Manager asked me to advise him.

Marabaraba in the donga
My school carried out a practical project with the community, building a bridge where our road crossed a small river. On the afternoons set aside for building work, many of the pupils worked hard carrying stones and bringing water for cement. But some of them hid in the donga, and played marabaraba. A villager complained to the chief: 'Morena, how

irresponsible and ill-disciplined children are nowadays. In any case why should children be involved in Food for Work projects?'

What is this subject?

I have just graduated from NTTC with Development Studies as my Higher Spec, and have persuaded the principal to let me introduce Development Studies with Form A next January. Other members of staff are very critical. 'What is this subject?' asks the history teacher. 'It's just bits and pieces of other subjects. The children need an academic discipline'. 'If Development Studies becomes successful' says the geography teacher, 'we shall have to give up teaching history and geography'. The principal is changing his mind. 'Perhaps we should wait for a few years,' he says. 'After all, Development Studies is much the same as history and geography isn't it?'

Resources

We introduced Development Studies three years ago. We have Units 1-3, and a few draft chapters of the others. I use my college notes to prepare lessons. We have no library, and as the school is in the mountains I cannot get to Maseru to borrow books. I asked the principal for money to buy some books for the school. Today she said to me: 'You can have M 25.00 to cover all your Development Studies expenses for next year'. I asked a colleague for sympathy. 'Even if you had more money' she said, 'You still wouldn't be able to find any useful books here in Lesotho'.

'Less important'

I have just finished my BEd at NUL taking Development Studies as my major. I returned to school this week, hoping and expecting to help my Development Studies colleague, who has classes of over 80 in Forms A and B. But when I saw the principal my hopes were dashed. 'You will be taking forms D and E for Sesotho and Geography, as you used to', he said. 'There is no one else to take them up to COSC. Since Development Studies can't be taken at COSC, it's less important for the future of our children'.

Why bother with the real thing?

I arranged for Form C to start a vegatable garden this year, so that they would be able to answer the compulsory question on the practical project in the JC exam. A delegation of pupils came to see me. 'We want to concentrate on the syllabus', they said. 'It's too late to do a project now. We can quite easily invent an imaginary project to write about in the exam, same as they did last year. Anyway, the examiner will be more impressed if we all write about different projects'.

Problems of development
For the topic 'problems of development', I planned a series of discussion lessons. After the first two I detected an uncooperative atmosphere in the class and I asked what the matter was. One girl spoke up. 'We don't want to discuss these problems', she said, 'We want to be told what the answers are, so that we can pass the exam'. Another said: 'It's difficult enough writing in English, let alone discussion. Why can't we discuss in Sesotho?'

Danger! Keep out!
I was going to this workshop on Development Studies and in the papers sent to me was a passage from a man called Paulo Freire. Something about 'knowledge necessitates the curious presence of subjects confronted with the world' — I couldn't make much sense of it, so I asked a friend about it. 'Oh', he said, 'that guy. Always talking about conscientising the masses, getting them to be more self-reliant and independent. I'd keep away from that workshop, if I were you'.

Re rutoa lipolitiki
In a lesson on 'forms of government', I explained the workings of the American Congress. Next day Lineo's father came up to the school and spoke to the Principal, who called me to his office. 'I understand', he said, 'that you have been spreading BCP propaganda. You must stop it at once'. Later that day I asked my younger sister, who is in Form B, what she thought of Development Studies at her school. She shrugged. 'Seems like it's teaching us we must obey the chiefs and vote for the government party', she said.

11. Talking as Equals
— the moral culture of the classroom

The previous essay, entitled How Learners Learn, *referred to structured discussion exercises, and to their advantages as alternatives to — though not complete replacements for — lectures and genuine discussion. Here now is an extended description of discussion exercises, and of their usefulness in school classrooms.*

The practical pedagogy proposed with the A-G-E-N-D-A mnemonic in How Learners Learn *was integrally linked to the theoretical account of different stances towards political power in* Learning toward Justice, *and the argument was that such a pedagogy is appropriate and indeed necessary if there is to be a possibility of learners choosing to adopt a 'transforming' stance towards power rather than a 'conforming' one.*

Similarly the argument here is that the moral climate which genuine discussion both requires and creates is one which is particularly relevant to education for equality — for in such a climate there is greater space for, and confidence amongst, the power-less; greater openness and tolerance of ambiguity and dissonance amongst the power-ful; and greater likelihood of genuine dialogue, negotiation and cooperation between power-less and power-ful, 'Davinder' and 'David', oppressed and oppressor.

* * * * *

From this lesson I've learnt that you have to work in a group to be able to achieve certain things...'

'I think I have learnt in this lesson how to listen to people very hard, and how to speak clearer, so that people can understand me.'

'From this lesson I've learnt that you've got to communicate if you want to get anywhere. It helps to work in groups, and problems are solved much more quickly in this way...'

'The lesson I think learnt us how to use our imagination, to invent things that may be stupid but isn't really stupid.'

Those comments were written by pupils at the end of a lesson. They had been asked to jot down what they thought they had learnt during the previous eighty minutes. This essay is about that particular lesson and, more generally and more importantly, about the assumptions and hopes behind it. The essay has three parts.

First, there is a brief description of the specific activities and exercises which were used. Second, there is a discussion of that general kind of lesson: what (hopefully) is going on beneath the surface, what are the principles behind it? Third, the style of teaching in that lesson is considered in relation to the general field of education for equality. In what ways may it be distinctively relevant to this field whose key concepts include justice, power, conflict, oppression, and which should be aiming, centrally, to oppose and dismantle inequalities?[1]

The lesson
First, the pupils formed small groups — four or five of them in each group. The first task in each group was extremely simple: in one minute make as long a list as you can of things present in this room. At the end of the minute, the items in each list were counted and briefly compared with each other. Then there was another minute for list-making, this time of things which were unlikely to be on any other group's list. Next, each group was given a paper-clip and asked to list all the possible uses they could think of for it. After that, every group made a list of famous people they would like to meet.

This making of lists without discussion is customarily known as brainstorming. It usefully creates the subject-matter for a discussion; it encourages everyone to participate, since there is no or little chance of anyone looking or feeling ridiculous; it provides a simple experience of cooperation and of open-mindedness within a small group; it promotes a lively and observant atmosphere, and a readiness to be imaginative, to engage in lateral thinking; it develops a basic self-confidence, within both individuals and small groups. It is an extremely humble activity in relation to the immense overall task of promoting greater social justice through education. It is not, however, wholly irrelevant.

On this occasion we used the fourth list, the one of famous people whom the pupils would like to meet, as a basis for discussion. Supposing they could only meet five of these people? Which five would these be? Supposing they could only meet four? Three? Two? One? The five were ranked, and each group's choices were read out in rank order.

Next, a 'jigsaw exercise'. Each group was given a strip cartoon which had been cut up into separate pictures. Each individual pupil had one picture, and could not see the pictures held by others. They had to describe their pictures to each other in order to work out what order they came in. Such an exercise is excellent for promoting close observation and careful mutual attention, and a sense that everyone has an important contribution to make. It was followed by another brainstorming exercise and by another selection exercise. The tasks this time were to brainstorm a list of possible titles for the cartoon strip story, and then to select from this list the title which the groups considered best.

Finally, the exercise known sometimes as 'Cooperation Squares' or 'Getting it Together'.[2] Normally, this is an exercise for groups of five. But on this occasion we had two groups of ten, plus several observers. Within each group of ten the pupils worked in pairs. Each pair had to make a square from pieces of cardboard. They could give and take pieces. No talking or sign language was allowed.

The lesson closed with the pupils being asked to write down what they thought they had learnt in the course of the lesson. The quotations at the start of this article were from their jottings. Here are one or two more:

'The lesson was very interesting, and not surprisingly everyone took part. I enjoyed working in groups, even better the way how we were made to think and write quickly. It also made me realise that although you may not be able to think or even write down your thoughts you did it when you were in groups.'

'In the lesson today we learnt how to work puzzles out by other peoples information. We were learnt how to use our minds and imaginations. It was good fun.'

'I think that this lesson was well worth having, because of the pleasure it brought me and the extra Education it taught me also.'

'I think that this lesson was quite good, it made us think of things quickly and it kept us aware all the time. I would look far more forward to coming to English for a double lesson if we had this every week. The class seemed to mix in and we talked more.'

That was just a one-off lesson, yes. It was not part of a series, and it did not have any content or subject-matter in the conventional sense. Not a great deal can be claimed for it — not for just that lesson on its own. But it *could* have been part of a series of lessons, and it *could* have been concerned with conventional subject-matter not only in English (it was officially an 'English' lesson) but also in most other subjects. It did illustrate a general approach to teaching, a general style. The multicultural classroom, as also any classroom engaging with issues of equality and racism, could — and it is to be argued here, should — be formed by that general approach and style.

There are numerous handbooks currently available for teachers, describing in detail the kinds of activity and exercise which we used in that lesson. Examples include handbooks produced from within the field of PSHE — personal social and health education;[3] handbooks concerned specifically with communication and language development, for example those developed by the English Language Institute of the British Council;[4] and handbooks intended for the field of world studies, the multicultural curriculum, development education, peace education.[5] It is important to identify the general principles behind such games and exercises. It is much easier to use them yourself, and to invent your own, if you feel reasonably comfortable with the theories in the background.

But first, an attempt at description rather than theorising. At the least we need a name for this general style of teaching. Experiential Learning? Structured Activities for Small Groups? Experience-Centred? Interactive? Dialogue? Participatory? Socio-Affective? Group Dynamics? Values Clarification?[6] Let us adopt here something reasonably simple, humble, sayable: *discussion exercises*. A teacher is using discussion exercises, let us say further, if some or all of the following features are present:

> If the pupils are working in small groups, normally with between two and six members, and if the group is the key unit so far as the teacher is concerned, not the individual pupil;

> if there is a specific outcome to be achieved by a specific time, and if groups achieve this outcome through discussion — that is, through the exchange of viewpoints and information;

> if there are certain rules of procedure which encourage or require all pupils to take part — in the ideal lesson built around discussion exercises, every individual pupil speaks more than the teacher speaks;

> if some sort of activity is required, however simple, in addition to talking, listening, writing, reading.

Lessons using discussion exercises are rather — or very — different from traditional lessons, for the latter normally involve the teacher doing the vast majority of the talking, and involve her hearing and controlling the vast majority of whatever talking the pupils do. But lessons using discussion exercises are not (or not necessarily) chaotic; they do not mean that the pupils are less attentive or less considerate; they do not necessarily promote 'chat' as distinct from 'talk', that is, conversation as distinct from debate. Certainly they are not merely permissive and 'progressive', not just wishy-washy and shoulder-shrugging liberalism, not just examples of the bland leading the bland. The distinction between chat and talk, or conversation and debate, is incidentally extremely important. All too often teachers and others assume that the only alternative to instruction by themselves or by textbooks and worksheets is desultory chat and conversation amongst pupils. But discussion is also a real alternative — *both* to instruction *and* to conversation:

> 'The central function of discussion is the improvement of knowledge, understanding and / or judgement... Discussion is not necessarily restricted...to the pursuit of truth (knowledge) but is an activity which can be associated with the illumination of alternatives in an area which does not admit of fully objective and rational conclusion;... with the evolution of judgement through mutual accommodation and adjustment of opinion rather than by straightforward reference to evidence and indeed in the absence of such evidence... Discussion differs from the social art of conversation in that what the talk is about is a matter of some serious importance...'[7]

On the next page is a list of practical tips for devising and using discussion exercises in the classroom. All of these tips are illustrated in the description of one particular lesson with which this essay began. Behind the tips, which are mainly technical rather than theoretical, there are three basic principles: first, the pupils are developing certain linguistic and conceptual skills; second, they are learning certain social skills in their relationships with each other; third, they are developing certain moral attitudes.

With regard to the first principle, regarding linguistic and conceptual skills, it is relevant to note a comment from the field of political education. 'All education whether in school or out of school consists of increasing understanding of language and increasing ability to use it..'[8] Par excellence, discussion involves increasing ability to use language — a wider and more flexible vocabulary, a greater capacity to make sense of new ideas, and to make them one's own. The Bullock Report, amongst other major documents and writing on language and concept development, has emphasised that the distinction between 'being told', for example by a teacher or a textbook or a worksheet, and 'finding out for oneself', for example through discussion, is a false one. You *cannot* be told something unless you first create for yourself a framework in which to receive it:

DISCUSSION EXERCISES — SOME PRACTICAL TIPS

Things to handle
Arrange for pupils to have things which are literally tangible — objects, pictures, slips of paper, which they can move around with their hands.

Precise task
Give precise instructions about what is to be done. For example: "Here are pictures of six different people. Choose the two people you would most like to meet. For each of them, write down the one question you would most like to ask."

Cooperation
Choose discussion tasks which require pupils to listen to each other and to help each other. For example, use "jigsaw games", which can only be completed if everyone takes part.

Small groups
The smaller the group, the more pupils feel secure. Also, the more they're able to talk. Often arrange for them to work in pairs or in threes. The maximum for most group work is six.

Controversy
Choose subjects on which pupils are likely to have conflicting opinions. Or build controversy into a discussion by requiring some of the participants to play specific roles.

Nonverbal material
Use material which communicates ideas symbolically and nonverbally rather than through words alone — photographs, cartoons, posters, statistical diagrams.

Comparing, contrasting, selecting, justifying
Provide a collection of things to be compared and contrasted with each other; require people to arrange them or to select from them; and to explain their arrangement or selection.

Activity then reflection
Give pupils an activity to perform, or require them to watch an activity — for example a nonverbal game or exercise. Then invite discussion and clarification of what happened, and of how they felt, and of what can be learnt.

Not too easy, not too hard
Definitely try to stretch pupils with discussion tasks you set. But don't depress them or annoy them by providing things which are too difficult. When you fail (as you sometimes will) to get the balance right, invite discussion of how people feel.

In order to accept what is offered when we are told something, we have to have somewhere to put it; and having somewhere to put it means that the framework of past knowledge and experience into which it must fit is adequate as a means of interpreting and apprehending it... The development of this individual context for a new piece of information, the forging of links that give it meaning, is a task that we customarily tackle by talking to other people.[9]

Discussion exercises help pupils to 'talk to other people', as Bullock puts it, and *therefore* to learn, to fit new ideas and information into their minds. But talking is not only a matter of moving your tongue, making a noise in other people's presence or company. It involves influencing other people as well as being influenced by them. The authors of a handbook for teachers on social skills itemise the following as necessary skills in small groups and one-to-one meetings:

— keeping it simple
— speaking clearly
— making and maintaining eye-contact
— monitoring others' responses
— giving consistent verbal and nonverbal signals
— being concrete
— summarising one's points every now and again
— checking out that others have understood[10]

All these skills are likely to be practised in discussion exercises. They are part of the higher-order skills of influencing a social situation or relationship, and achieving within it a sense of one's own identity and value. Pupils are most unlikely 'to talk to other people', as Bullock puts it, unless they are also able to influence and control other people or, at the very least, to resist being influenced and controlled by others in ways which they do not wish. This point is beautifully emphasised at one stage in Bernard Ashley's novel A *Kind of Wild Justice*.[11] Ronnie goes to remedial reading lessons in which the teacher tries to get him to talk and write about, as she calls it, real life. Ronnie's father was picked up last week by the police:

"Now, what can we write to make the book real, and exciting, and *yours?*" Her eyes shone at him.

"Dunno."

"Well think, Ronnie: you haven't thought." There was a long silence while Ronnie waited to be told. They always told you in the end.

"Well... it'd make a real book if you wrote something about your dad."

Like what? Like "My dad hates me because I got him nicked"? Would that bloody do her? He scowled, but he waited. She'd start writing something in a minute; then he could copy it underneath.

"Well, what about a short sentence like 'My Dad's gone away'? You see, being real, it might be more help than cards, and books; you can see how reading is part of life." He shrugged. At least it wasn't too long to copy. And who cares what the rotten words said? They were *nothing*.

Ronnie's teacher has read her Bullock Report, it can (alas) be assumed. Well anyway they told her about it at college, or at some inservice course or other. But she has not yet grasped that people don't talk to each other, therefore do not learn, unless there is a chance of controlling and influencing each other, and of resisting control and influence by each other. This is partly a matter of social skills — what the authors of the handbook cited earlier describe as 'assertive' behaviour as distinct both from 'aggressive' and 'non-assertive'. (Bernard Ashley's novel, incidentally, is about whether a growing child can be assertive, not aggressive and also not non-assertive, within the criminal sub-culture of the East End.) But it is not only a matter of social skills. Also, it is a matter of morality, of moral education.

In the book on discussion already cited, the author speaks of 'the moral culture of group discussion'. If pupils are really to engage in discussion — not conversation, and not mere battles for control and influence — there needs to be an atmosphere of 'reasonableness' 'peaceableness and orderliness', 'truthfulness', 'freedom' and 'respect for persons'. A necessary but not sufficient condition for such an atmosphere is a set of rules with which everyone complies. (Preferable to compliance, of course, is active, willing, conscious, intentional acceptance, and joint responsibility with the teacher for maintaining the rules.) Discussion exercises, it is important to note, can contribute to the moral culture of group discussion: they can contribute, though not guarantee.

Discussion exercises have the same relationship to moral culture as, in everyday life, good manners have to consideration and love. They are both a sign and a signpost, both a mirror and a mould. As it were, they both simulate and stimulate: they simulate the good society, perfect equality and democracy, what Habermas calls the 'ideal speech situation' in which everyone has identical 'communicative competence'[12] and also they act as a stimulus, provoking us to make real that which we pretend. So to speak, they are outward and visible signs of a faith: 'only by virtue of faith does dialogue have power and meaning: by faith in people and their possibilities, by the faith that I can only become truly myself when other people also become themselves'.[13]

Discussion exercises simulate and stimulate moral culture by requiring participants to see both themselves and each other in a particular way: as centres of consciousness, subjects who can and do say 'I', with wishes, intentions, hopes, ideals; they are not objects to be manipulated, not empty vessels to be given 'inputs'. (This common term 'imput' surely implies a terrible failure in understanding and in moral respect on the part of many teachers and conference organisers.) If people attend to you as someone from whom they can learn, you feel valued, sure of yourself, secure. You feel that you for your part can dare to attend to others — that is, to risk being challenged and changed by them, by what they know, by how they think and see. This is important for teacher-pupil relationships, it is worth emphasising, as well as for relationships amongst pupils.

Education for equality

Discussion exercises are relevant, it has in effect been argued here, for the whole field of social and political education and for that of moral education. Arguably they also have a distinctive contribution to make to the sub-field within these two larger fields which is marked by terms such as multicultural education, world studies, development education, and so on. There are three main points: discussion exercises are a response to 'structural violence' within educational institutions; they contribute directly to the dismantling and unlearning of racism in multicultural classrooms and schools; they promote interest in the wider world, for example in cultures and countries other than one's own, and in issues of conflict, justice and racial equality.

The concept of structural violence was developed in the 1960s by peace researchers in order to emphasize that a ceasefire, a cessation of overt violence, is not an absolute value. A society or community can live 'in peace' with its neighbours or its enemies but can be so structured inwardly, or its relationships with others can be so structured, that significant numbers of people are dying young, or are living cramped, oppressed, unfulfilled lives. Similarly a society can achieve 'racial harmony', at least temporarily, without achieving the far more important value of racial justice. Educational systems and practices may not only fail to challenge structural violence but may also in various ways actually reflect and reinforce it. This happens in the micro situation of the individual classroom, and in the individual school or college, as well as in a regional or national educational system as a whole.[14]

Changes in the micro situation of the individual classroom, for example through the use of discussion exercises and through the creation of the kind of miniature democracy which such exercises (to repeat) both simulate and stimulate, do little or nothing to challenge structural violence and institutionalised racism elsewhere. But at least they are worth making. They mean that at least one is not colluding with the overall system; and they may well have a beneficial influence in at least the individual institution, making it more responsive and flexible — 'a school as if people really mattered', with teachers respecting their pupils as capable of asking their own questions, and of caring and reasoning responsibly about the major social issues of our times.[15] Certainly it seems idle to promote 'a world community' or 'a democratic and participatory multi-racial society' without seeking to bring these concepts alive — these concepts of community, democracy, participation, equality — in each individual classroom, and without enhancing teachers' images and expectations of their pupils.

A second point is that discussion exercises may be particularly valuable in heterogeneous classrooms: mixed attainment, mixed social class, co-educational, a mixture of 'races', cultures and languages. This is partly due to their equalising function: they require or encourage eveyone to take part as equals.[16] Partly also it is because discussion exercises can be devised which both reflect the diversity already present in a classroom and build on it. Diversity is then seen as a resource rather than a problem. For example, it is sometimes possible and desirable for pupils who all belong to the same cultural background to work together in discussion exercises, and they can be encouraged to speak to each other in their first language.

Third, discussion exercises help pupils to take a more lively and positive interest in the wider world. There is an important paradox at work here: just as it is difficult or impossible to attend to others if they do not for their part attend to yourself, so it is difficult for a group to empathise with other groups, and to care for them and trust them, until it has first established mutual respect and trust amongst its own members. The distinction between 'internal' and 'external' relationships with foreigners is relevant here.[17] With internal relationships you see foreigners as 'living persons with goals and intentions' who are 'in the process of developing', or who 'possess an innate potential to develop'. With external relationships you see foreigners as jetsam on the sea of history, 'determined by external causes rather than by their own desires and objectives'. You cannot have internal relationships with foreigners if you have external relationships with the people close to you: discussion exercises arguably break down external relationships in the classsroom itself. Further, they enhance the self-esteem both of individual pupils and of groups. There is evidence from a wide range of psychological research that high self-esteem is a necessary condition for interest in, and knowledge about, other countries and cultures, and for commitment to racial equality and social justice.[18]

Consider again young Ronnie, for example, the hero of Bernard Ashley's novel. As long as he is unsure of his own identity, and distrustful both of himself and of all adults whom he knows, he sees Manjit Kaur, the other pupil in his withdrawal group for remedial reading, as a mere 'Paki', for the most part to be ignored but sometimes to be manipulated, threatened, literally kicked and pushed around. But as he slowly comes to trust himself, as a result of being trusted and attended to by others, he glimpses that Manjit is a human being as well, with fears and loves and intentions, not just a stereotype. Equally he glimpses an alternative to the subculture into which he has been born, the subculture of, in one character's words. 'force and violence, the law of the jungle grovelling to the strongest'. He glimpses a social order of real equality, real justice.

A social order characterised by racial equality and justice is a long way away in Britain. It will certainly not be created, to repeat and emphasise, by discussion exercises in school classrooms nor, indeed, by changes in education alone. But *one* arena for struggle is the school classroom itself, and the use of language in classrooms. Building equal communicative competence in the classroom — between pupil and pupil, and pupil and teacher — is one honourable task, amongst others. It needs to be complemented and supported by very many other initiatives: yes of course. But to engage in it is important, indeed vital. Such engagement may be inspired by the motto and the vision of one of the twentieth century's greatest freedom movements: 'there is no way to equality; equality is the way'. [19] Yes, an honourable task.

12. Truths About Bias
— a decalogue for Monday morning

The previous two essays, How Learners Learn *and* Talking as Equals, *have outlined respectively the agenda and the culture which are desirable in the everyday school classroom if learner-centred education and education for equality are to be successfully implemented. They have not referred, however, to the fact that the teacher who tries to implement these ideals in practice is bound to have to handle with pupils various issues which are controversial — that is, in a simple but very serviceable definition, issues on which society is divided. Amongst other things, handling such issues is likely to involve having to cope with allegations that one is 'indoctrinating' not 'educating'.*

This piece was written in Lesotho, Southern Africa, between about midnight and two o'clock in the morning, on a Sunday night. On the Monday I would be introducing, and then throughout the coming week I would be running, a workshop for teachers of development studies. The workshop would be patterned according to the A-G-E-N-D-A mnemonic, and would begin with a series of discussion exercises, of the kind described here in the essay entitled Talking as Equals. *I wrote the piece for a journal in England, and was using the middle of the night in order to get the manuscript into the post before the workshop began, and thus to meet the editors' deadline.*

But also, I was writing a kind of private aide-memoire, or even a set of firm instructions to myself, as I prepared to work with the teachers of development studies. For those teachers, close to the obscenities of apartheid but in a landlocked country dependent in all sorts of ways on the political and economic arrangements in the Republic surrounding them, ideas of oppression and potential liberation were far more vivid and concrete as daily realities than such ideas are for most teachers in Britain.Also, those teachers in Lesotho were in real danger of losing their livelihood, and perhaps worse, if they made errors of political judgement in their teaching. This piece thus constituted a meditation on my own moral responsibilities, as a visiting educator from a relatively comfortable and secure place, whilst I was amongst them.

* * * * *

Now', he said 'do we have any racial discrimination in Brackenhead? Do we? Who can tell me? Jane?'

The scene was a secondary school classroom which I happened to visit recently. I shall recount the episode faithfully, though also — I must admit — selectively. (I have, in a word, a bias.) It went as follows:

> '...Jane? Come on Jane, you heard the question, do we have any racial discrimination in Brackenhead?'
> *'Yes sir.'*
> 'Have we Jane? Have we really?'
> *'No sir.'*
> 'You're quite right, Jane, good, we have no racial discrimination in...'
> *'Sir.'*
> 'What is it Jane?'
> *'Sir.'*
> 'Come on Jane, what is it?'
> *'Sir, there's this Pakkie grocer near us and last Saturday night someone threw a brick through his window.'*
> 'Oh, I see, well, tell me Jane, er, what sort of person would do that?'
> *'Dunno, Sir.'*
> 'Jane, would you say that it was a very nasty, mean-minded, prejudiced sort of a person?'
> *'Yes Sir.'*
> 'Good, Jane, yes you're quite right.'

After the lesson I went with the teacher to the staffroom. 'We've just had,' he said to a colleague, 'a really good discussion about race relations.' I said nothing. There was no way, on the spur of the moment, I could find words which were both true and kind, or not untrue and not hurtfully destructive. This article, however, outlines what I was dimly and dumbly thinking. It is written for three separate reasons: to clarify my own ideas; as a resource for other educators who are sometimes at a loss for words; and to invite criticism and denial.

That lesson at Brackenhead contained four main kinds of bias. First, it was promoting an appallingly superficial and inadequate view of key concepts such as discrimination. Second, it was assuming a very impoverished and unthinking view of the nature of knowledge and learning. Third, it was implicitly presenting an obnoxious view of the role and authority of teachers. Fourth, it was propagating a false view about the nature of bias itself. In many ways this was the most pernicious bias of all and it is primarily this fourth kind of bias that I am going to write about here.

The teacher believed himself to be biased in the only way that nice, decent, well-intentioned people such as teachers *can* be biased. It was his professional duty, he believed, to present his views, since they were the consensus views of all right-thinking people, to his pupils. He was wrong.

Or rather, I think he was wrong. I should like to present my own views on the nature of bias in education, and the role and responsibility of educators, in the form of ten commandments.

Never forget there's a war on

There are objective conflicts of interest between white and black, North and South, ruler and worker, male and female, oppressor and oppressed. You cannot avoid taking sides. Any attempt to be neutral, even-handed, objective, will promote the interests of the stronger, of the oppressor. This is because there is no such thing as final objectivity, there is only unending struggle. Your commitment should be first of all to justice, not to 'truth'.

Pursue truth as a duty, not as a virtue

Facts should be accurate, not fake or distorted, and you should always be on your guard against fantasy and wishful thinking: the world is not made in your image and it is not made for your sole convenience. However, do not congratulate yourself on making accurate statements as distinct from lies or guesses or hopeful estimates, or on seeing and understanding reality independently of your personal preferences. Accuracy and honesty should be pursued as a matter of course, not as a matter of pride.

Never say or imply that your own view is the only view

The besetting sin of liberals is to assume that all decent people are liberals, and that only extremists have non-liberal views. The assumption and promotion of consensus are always, in themselves, wrong. Sometimes the consensus view is the best view, but always remember that it is the consensus view *because* it is the best view; it is never the best view because it is the consensus view. In particular you should never forget, as a teacher, that there are *always* more radical views than your own. For teachers necessarily and inherently have to uphold certain conventions and traditions. You are deceiving your pupils if you permit them to believe that there are no thoughtful, knowledgeable and responsible people more radical than yourself.

Do not caricature or ridicule your opponents

Your opponents are not only wrong but also tiresome and, quite probably, malevolent. Nevertheless you should resist the temptation to dehumanise them — that is, to simplify them for cheap laughs, to change them into symbols, into generalisations, into objects to be tossed around and tossed away. Engage your opponents with due respect. State their views more accurately and more persuasively than they state them themselves. Then argue and demonstrate — do not merely say — that they are wrong.

Protect people from your own powers of persuasion

If and when your pupils see the world in the same way as you do, this must be because they have freely chosen to engage on the same side as you against injustice. It must not be because they are dazzled by your charisma or oratory, or because you have rewards with which to woo them, or punishments with which to coerce them. True, you must be skilful and crafty and artful — as distinct from incompetent, inarticulate, inelegant. But you may not be manipulative, you may not cast spells. Use your skill to prevent your pupils from being taken in by your skill.

Acknowledge your own doubts and your own search

You haven't always held the views you hold now. You will not always hold them in their present form in the future. You cannot be sure that you are right — even though, certainly, you can be reasonably sure that certain other people are wrong. You must hunger and thirst after more knowledge, and your pupils must see this. Continually you should seek to be criticised and challenged, to be put to the test. 'I cannot praise a cloistered virtue,' said Milton. You should say the same, and your pupils should hear you.

Link facts to theories

A fact is a fact is a fact: yes of course. But facts as such are profoundly uninteresting and trivial. Facts are significant — they are worth knowing and communicating and researching — only within the context of theories. Theories, unlike facts, are not right or wrong. Rather, they approximate more or less closely to reality and they promote more or less effectively greater social justice. This is what you should help your pupils to see. Insofar as you fail, your pupils will end up watching Mastermind on television, and other mindless quiz programmes, which similarly obscure and falsify reality, and contain and deaden the struggle for social justice.

Provide space and time

You wish your pupils to see the world more clearly and to pursue justice more vigorously. Amongst other things their learning will therefore involve unlearning — discarding what they already know, or think they know. This is painful. Poincaré had all the information he needed to see the theory of relativity. But he did not dare put it together, his mind could not unlearn the connections it had already made. We had to wait for Einstein — he dared to unlearn. If your pupils are to break up their present world they need space and time — your job as teacher is to provide and protect that space and time. Hold the ring and guard the door, and they will learn, and unlearn, all right.

Ask questions

Or rather, make sure that your pupils ask questions. They should criticise and challenge, they should find all things questionable and problematic. This is not to say they should be like the quizmasters on television — questions in themselves are as perniciously pointless as facts in themselves. Rather, they should know reality is only grasped and only altered — oppression is only combated — when human beings are questioning as distinct from accepting.

Don't start other people's revolutions

Real learning is painful and that is bad enough. It leads into conflict and therefore perhaps defeat, and that is worse. You may not as a teacher go around stirring up revolutions — in families, in peer groups, in institutions, in societies — from which you yourself will be absent and in which, therefore, you yourself will not be hurt. Your pupils are to engage in war and revolution, yes, but not as cannon-fodder with yourself as armchair strategist. Your job as teacher is quite humble: to equip your pupils to identify and to fight battles they can win.

If that teacher at Brackenhead were to heed and obey such commandments his classroom and his pupils — and his work and his life — would be very different. If I myself abided by them more faithfully I would surely have found some words for him at that appalling moment when he claimed to have been engaging his pupils in discussion. Still, there is now this essay.

What will be the effect if — no, my brothers and sisters, *when* — that teacher reads it?

13. Caring and Not Caring
— stories on the seashore

'Don't try to teach a pig to sing,' said a teacher once. 'It's a waste of your time. And it irritates the pig.' Her advice is included in an anthology of sayings by various anonymous teachers over the centuries, made by the Indian writer Anthony de Mello. The title of the anthology is One Minute Wisdom. Though isn't a minute rather too brief a space of time, wonders de Mello in his introduction, in which to attain wisdom? No, he replies to his own question, it is fifty-nine seconds too long. For whilst 'opening one's eyes may take a lifetime, seeing is done in a flash.'

The teachers in de Mello's anthology belong to a variety of cultures, traditions and periods, but have in common that their educational purposes are evoked with terms such as 'awakening' and 'enlightenment', yet also 'detachment' and 'renunciation', and that their characteristic teaching method is the use of story, metaphor, parable and paradox: 'the shortest distance between a human being and Truth is a story', says one of them, and another: 'Do not despise the story. A lost gold coin is found by means of a penny candle; the deepest truth is found by means of a simple story.' They have in common too that they are ready, though with great carefulness and a certain diffidence, to use words such as 'God', 'the divine', 'spirit' and 'spiritual'.

This essay recalls some of the aspirations and methodology of such teaching, and considers the possibility that mainstream education, and in particular education for equality, may have much to learn from it. For if you are involved in the exhausting politics and politicking of trying to build greater equality and justice in education, it is particularly urgent that you should strike a balance between attachment and detachment. A certain detachment — a certain 'not caring' is essential for movement itself: consider, says famously and hauntingly one of de Mello's teachers in One Minute Wisdom, the relationship between birds in flight and the lake beneath them: 'they cast their reflection on the water without knowing, and without knowing the water receives it.'

This essay began life as a lecture to an audience of headteachers and religious education specialists, at a conference organised by Ealing Community Relations Council. It included in its original version a story for headteachers in particular, adapted from a brief tale in One Minute Wisdom, which bears repeating here: A headteacher went for guidance from a spiritual teacher. — 'As the fish perishes on dry land,' said the spiritual teacher, 'so you perish when you get entangled in your school. The fish must return to the water, and you must return to solitude.' — 'What?' replied the headteacher aghast. 'Must I give up my school and go into the desert, or into a religious community somewhere?'— 'No,' was the answer. 'Hold on to your school. But go into the cave of your heart.'

* * * * *

Teach us, runs part of a prayer in *Ash Wednesday* by T S Eliot, to care and not to care. The yearning is to live vibrantly with a historic and universal tension: between attachment and detachment, desiring and renouncing, seizing and letting go, holding and giving away.

We experience the tension in many different spheres and aspects of our lives — our lives as, amongst others, lover, parent, worker, politician, artist, teacher. A term to describe an aspect of what we need, if we are to cope productively with the tension, is 'spiritual direction'. This essay recalls some of the main features of spiritual direction, specifically those which are relevant to the tension between engagement and disengagement in political life and endeavour, and reflects on various practical implications for teaching, and for the curriculum of schools. Its overall pattern is as follows.

First, a traditional folktale recalls the basic tension between engagement and withdrawal, and discussion of its various possible interpretations introduces the notion that prayer and meditation (withdrawal) may be as important, in the overall task of building and maintaining new power relations in society at large, as politics and economics (engagement). Second, a handful of teachings about prayer and meditation are recollected, and there are notes on the relationships which spiritual teachers over the centuries have suggested between the respective concerns of ashram and action, desert and deed, prayer and politics, silence and struggle, spirituality and society. Third, there is a brief list of practical implications for mainstream schools and classrooms in the formal education system. These relate most obviously to the subject-area known as religious education, but are more widely relevant to many other subject areas also: spiritual development, to cite a term which appears right at the start of the Education Reform Act, is after all a cross-curricular concern. It is related to, but emphatically is not the same as, moral development and personal development. The essay draws to a close by noting some possible objections to its thesis that mainstream education should be concerned with, amongst other things, spiritual development, in the sense that this term is understood in the world's traditions of teaching about prayer and meditation; and it concludes with some beautiful words about engagement and detachment, and about passion and playfulness, by Rabindranath Tagore. It is from these that the image in the essay's sub-title is taken: 'children have their play,' said Tagore, 'on the seashore of worlds.'

Throughout the essay there is a tacit assumption that the tension between attachment and detachment has its analogues in the tension between west and east, and for example therefore in the tensions between Anglo-Saxon and Indian, and Hindu and Christian. 'Many Christians,' it has been suggested, 'tend to be too involved in history, in work, in service to suffering humanity. . . The Hindu, on the other hand, does not realise sufficiently the reality of the human person, of his sufferings, of his destiny, and that life has an ultimate purpose. It is not just a *lila*, a play. . .We are always swinging between these two poles. We have to find an equilibrium. There is no simple answer . . . This is one of the places where Hindu and Christian have to meet together and work together. We must learn from one another. That is the secret.'[1]

The 'marriage' of east and west, feminine and masculine, Indian and Anglo-Saxon, Hindu and Christian, is a marriage also, to recall a metaphor from earlier in this book (in the piece entitled *Stages and Stances*), between Davinder and David, oppressed and oppressor. It has a deeply significant role to play, therefore, in all political action and campaigning to build equality and justice.

The Five Teachers
An urgent call came to the great Lama of the north from the Lama of the south, asking for a wise and holy teacher to be sent to initiate young people in the south into the nature and contours of the spiritual life. To everyone's astonishment the great Lama sent five teachers instead of one. To those who asked why he replied cryptically : 'We shall be fortunate if one of them gets to the Lama of the south.'

The group of five set off. They had been on the road for several days when a messenger came running up to them and cried: 'There is a terrible famine in our village, the rains and the crops have failed, both beasts and people are starving, many have already died. Abide with us, we pray you, care for us, teach us knowledge of wholeness, of the earth, of nature.' — 'I would not be a Buddhist,' said one of the five teachers sent by the Lama of the north, 'if I did not stop here, and provide knowledge and assistance for these suffering people.' The other four continued.

A few days later the four came to a city where some of the people on the streets exclaimed urgently to them: 'This place is corrupt, the system of this city is oppressive, capricious, uncaring, cruel. Stay with us here, we pray you, and help us to resist and to replace the rulers of this city, and to govern ourselves in justice and in peace.' — 'I would not be a Buddhist,' said one of the teachers sent by the Lama of the north, 'if I did not stop here, and join in resistance, politics and government.' The other three continued.

Some days later the three came to a town where there was much discord and argument amongst members of different religious groups. 'Help us, we pray you,' said some of the people, 'to understand and to tolerate each other's festivals and customs. So that each person here is grounded in their own tradition and history, but is respectful of the traditions and histories of others.' — 'I would not be a Buddhist,' said one of the teachers sent by the Lama of the north, 'if I did not stop here, and help to promote order and tolerance.' The other two continued.

A few days later the two came to a small settlement where there were many children playing in vigorous peace. There were dances and games, paintings and music, embraces and laughter. There was ripening fruit on the trees, there were solid houses and homes. 'Settle with us here, we pray you,' said the people, 'set up home, enjoy sexual love, nurture and cherish new human beings, join us here in building the future.' — 'I would not be a Buddhist,' said one of the teachers sent by the Lama of the north, 'if I did not stop and make my dwelling here, and live in passionate and birthing love with kin and neighbours.' The other went on.

Eventually the fifth teacher reached the Lama of the south, and began there the work which had been requested, and which was required, that of initiating young people into the nature and contours of the spiritual life.[2]

At first sight, as we wonder about possible interpretations of this story, we perhaps see it as belonging to the familiar genre of pilgimage-with-temptations story. Question, how do you get to heaven? Answer, with difficulty, for there are so many distractions and temptations along the way. All five set out singing 'here we go', but only one stays the course

137

to say 'here I am' at the end: four of them get lost, even though in very important and splendid good causes, and only one really understands the true nature of the spiritual life. Another interpretation involves placing the story in the genre of a stages-of-life narrative. It is then about the values of science and rationality; of politics and justice; of tolerance and tradition; of sexual and family life. Only after these four sets of values have been realised, though not necessarily in that order, is it appropriate to devote oneself, like a Hindu sannyasi, to a life apart, a life of renunciation and contemplation.

A third interpretation involves situating the story in the genre of a God-incognito narrative. There are many such stories in all religious traditions, with their recurring and typical emphasis that God plays hide-and-seek with human beings by mischievously incarnating herself in secular and ordinary situations, and in persons in need. God is then encountered not in holy slots removed from political and personal life but only in interaction and involvement with other people. 'If I could persuade myself,' said Mahatma Gandhi, 'that I could find God in a Himalayan cave I would proceed there immediately. But I know that I cannot find him apart from humanity.'[3]

A fourth kind of interpretation would see the story as being about the tension between caring and not caring. In this interpretation the Lama of the north sends, as it were, five persons in one individual. The first four teachers represent attachment and involvement of various kinds within a single person — all of us, according to this interpretation, need to be applied scientists, to be involved in government and in the main-tenance of order and tolerance, to have vibrant personal relationships — and the fifth teacher represents the need for withdrawal. Unless the fifth is present within each individual there is the danger of frenetic and self-indulgent activism, leading eventually to burn-out and despair. There is the danger too of religion coming to serve purely temporal and secular interests, and of becoming an opiate. Thomas Merton writes in this connection:

> When religion becomes a mere artificial facade to justify a social and economic system — when religion hands over its rites and language completely to the political propagandist, and when prayer becomes the vehicle for a purely secular ideological pro-gram, then religion does tend to become an opiate.... This brings

about the alienation of the believer, so that religious zeal becomes political fanaticism. Faith in God, while preserving its traditional formulas, becomes in fact faith in one's own nation, class or race.[4]

Merton observes that religion becomes thus distorted and narrowed down to supporting a nation, class or race when it loses contact with its own traditions of prayer and contemplation, and in particular loses contact with what he calls the uselessness of such traditions: 'it is the contemplative, silent, "empty" and apparently useless element in the life of prayer which makes it truly a life.' If Christians are to rediscover the uselessness of prayer, they need to be open to learnings and insights in other religious traditions. This is particularly appropriate and logical, and indeed probably absolutely necessary, if they intend to resist and to confront those various tendencies in contemporary culture, nurtured both by the tabloid press and the New Right, to equate Christianity with whiteness and Britishness.[5]

A fifth approach would be to find in the story a recapitulation, though with a certain poetic licence with regard to strict historical sequence, of the history of religious education in Britain between about 1960 and 1990. In the late 1950s the five teachers set out in order to teach about the Bible and Christianity: this was the goal of their journey, so they thought. But they were waylaid by a series of other priorities: teenage religion (Loukes) and childhood religion (Goldman) required, they decided, that they should teach about humanitarian good works and about personal identity; later, they embraced development education and political education; then were into social, personal and health education. Insofar as they genuinely engaged in something which might be reasonably called religious education this was to do with phenomenology, and the promotion of tolerance and pluralism, as in the Lancaster and Shap projects of the 1970s, and as strongly recommended in the Swann Report in the 1980s. The fifth teacher, in this interpretation, is perhaps then the solid evangelising Christian who has remained faithful to the end, and who will now, with the support of the Education Reform Act, return to the proselytising and nurturing priorities and assumptions of the 1950s. Alternatively and preferably, the fifth teacher represents a new possibility for the 1990s — someone who takes us on from personal and social education, and on also from the dry phenomenology of the Swann Report, and yet who is not indifferent to that broad tradition of religious education which is concerned with spiritual development as distinct from other kinds of development.

A sixth approach to interpreting the story therefore involves asking what the fifth teacher will actually do on arrival with the Lama of the south: what will be the content of the teaching, and what methods will be used? An immediate answer to the question about teaching method is that very probably multi-layered and ambiguous stories will be used, stories with multiple interpretations. Such stories, when told within a religious context, imply that there is a correspondence between three separate kinds of human capacity for insight and detachment:

> (i) the capacity to see and hear the meaning of a story — pennies drop not only when there is insight (eyes to see, ears to hear) but also when there's a readiness to be detached, to renounce and let go of the irritable striving to control and to be certain, a readiness to live with mystery and with unresolved questions;

> (ii) the capacity to live attentively and caringly with other human beings, both in everyday personal relationships and in political action to build and to defend justice in social affairs — this too involves insight (in this instance, insight into others' needs and realities and into appropriate political strategies), and at the same time a certain peaceful detachment and unknowing, a readiness to let other people choose and go their own pathways, a readiness to live with mystery and unresolved questions;

> (iii) the capacity to see and to hear 'God' (inverted commas since many religious stories recall that God frequently and typically goes playfully unrecognised, and therefore unnamed) — and this too involves not only eyes to see and ears to hear but also a certain peaceful unknowing, a readiness to renounce and let go, a readiness to live with mystery and unresolved questions.

Yes surely, the teacher will amongst other things be telling stories. A contemporary writer has defined theology as 'the art of telling stories about the Divine'. And mysticism as 'the art of tasting and feeling in your heart the inner meaning of such stories to the point that they transform you.'[6]

The purposes and subject-matter of spiritual teaching can be evoked with stories from around the world's religious traditions about prophet and guru, roshi and sage, sister and monk, rabbi and mullah. For example there is the famous story of the time when God sought advice from such a person. 'I want,' said God, 'to play a game of hide-and-seek with humankind. I have asked my angels where would be the best place to conceal myself. Some say in the depths of the deepest ocean. Others on the tip of the highest mountain. Others again on the far side of the moon. Where do you suggest ?' Said the spiritual teacher: 'Hide in the human heart, that's the last place they will think of looking.'

Or there is that story of the three sisters. When they were grown up each decided to seek God in her own way. The first declared: 'I'm going to look after the sick and broken, the streets are full of them, I will bring them healing and care.' The second: 'Everywhere I see people in dispute and conflict with one another. I will go out to reconcile them, I will bring them peace.' The third sister declared that she would stay at home. After two years the first two sisters returned. The first said: 'It's hopeless, there are simply too many sick people, I cannot cope.' The second said much the same: 'It's impossible, I'm torn to shreds.' They sat in exhausted and burnt-out despair, looking at each other.

Then the third sister filled a bowl with muddy water from a nearby pool. 'Look into that,' she said. 'Look.' They looked but saw nothing, only muddy water. 'Let it stand,' she said, 'let it be.' After a while they looked again. The water was clear now, and they saw their own reflections in it, as clearly as in a mirror The third sister told them: 'When the water is stirred up it is muddy and you can see nothing. It is clear only when it is very still. It is the same with us human beings. You can see clearly only when you are still, very still. Only when in stillness you see your own self can you see also what you should do, where you should go. Only then can you have hope and faith in the future, and in the worth-whileness of political endeavour, and in your own giftedness, grace and creativity. Only then can you plunge, with passionate love, into caring for others, whether through medicine or through politics. Only then can you be indifferent to rewards, indifferent to the fruits of action.'

So this is one thing, perhaps the first thing, which the teacher will do on arrival with the Lama of the south: teach the novices to be still and silent, and in stillness and silence to know themselves. Not caring about the world, but caring about silence. Being useless, not useful. Out of such stillness may grow hope and joy and determination, and faith that all manner of thing shall be well, which is a political as well as a personal faith. With such faith they may then go out and join, or alternatively stay in seclusion and pray for, the other four teachers and their immersion in politics and practicalities. It is the faith underlying action which is important, from this point of view, not the fruits of action. It is a faith based on seeing the external world objectively, uncoloured and unfashioned by one's own projections, preferences, wishful feelings, resentments, self-pityings, fabrications, one's own buffetings and wounds from involvement in practical and political affairs.

Prayer, spiritual stories and teachings repeatedly emphasise, is not in the first instance about being holy, or special, or 'good', but about knowing and being yourself. To cite Thomas Merton again:

> *Do not*
> *Think of what you are*
> *Still less of*
> *What you may one day be.*
> *Rather*
> *Be what you are (but who?) be*
> *The unthinkable one*
> *You do not know.*[7]

Contrast this with the view of prayer held by Rex in Evelyn Waugh's *Brideshead Revisited*. Father Mowbray has been appointed to instruct Rex in the Roman Catholic faith, so that Rex can marry Julia Marchmain. 'He's the most difficult convert I have ever met,' says Father Mowbray. 'I can't get anywhere near him. He doesn't seem to have the least intellectual curiosity or natural piety. The first day I wanted to find out what sort of religious life he had had up till now, so I asked him what he meant by prayer. He said: *I* don't mean anything. *You* tell me. I tried to in a few words, and he said, Right. So much for prayer. What's the next thing?'[8] There is no next thing, reply spiritual teachers in all traditions; prayer is as endless as life, prayer is endless exploration. Prayer, like politics, is an endless wrestling between hope and despair, perseverance and burn-out; it is an endless struggle to know oneself and others to be gifted and graceful; an endless search and re-search for blessing, for knowing one's own body and all the earth to be good, for being erotically committed to social justice and to the worthwhileness of political endeavour. For both attachment and detachment, both caring and not caring.

Not that knowledge of one's own goodness and gracefulness is the only knowledge to be gained in prayer! Meditating on the Buddhist ideal of Kannon, the enlightened person who listens to the cries and sufferings of all the world, a contemporary spiritual teacher writes: 'As I listen, listen, listen, I discover within myself the violence and hatred and anger that is shaking the world outside. It is inside and outside, within and around. I see my own appalling capacity for evil. I am a mirror that reflects the suffering and evil of the world.'[9] Hope and faith that all manner of things shall be well comes, if it does come, inspite of and in addition to such awareness, not through denial of it. In the absence of such awareness, political action to engage with negatives in the outer world is likely to be at best ineffective and draining and at worst actually harmful.

The life of wrestling towards enlightenment, and hopeful confidence in self and world, involves words, images, ikons, visualising, journalling, actions, chants, stories, koans, parables, riddles, music, candles, incense, physical exercise, attention to breathing and posture, mantras and mandalas, creeds and doctrines, silence: there are many, many techniques in the repertoire of the spiritual teacher — plenty, for example, to keep that teacher busy amongst the young people of the Lama of the south. These practical techniques and methods are both essential and totally unimportant, and towards these too an attitude of both caring and not caring is called for. 'What action shall I perform to attain God?' asked the disciple. 'If you wish to attain God,' replied the teacher, 'there are two things which you must know. The first is that all efforts to attain him are of no avail.' — 'And the second?' — 'You must act as if you did not know the first.'[10] The spiritual life is a kind of game, of playfulness: 'on the seashore of endless worlds,' said Tagore, 'is the great meeting of children.'

It is interesting to consider the actual practicalities of applying the techniques and methods of spiritual direction to the mainstream school classroom. The following implications are immediately obvious:

1) Teaching techniques of relaxation ('it takes a lot of doing to do nothing'); this will certainly include attention to breathing and posture, and possibly also the use of mantras; there is no reason why the latter should have a specifically religious reference or should be predicated on any specific religious doctrine.[11]

2) Teaching visualising techniques, and taking pupils on guided fantasies; these can include dialoguing inwardly with people whom they know, or whom they have met in dreams or in literature or on television, and can of course lead to various kinds of narrative writing.[12]

3) Teaching pupils to explore and to interpret parables, riddles, fables, paradoxes, wisdom tales, symbolic stories, metaphors, proverbs; such exploration and interpretation can involve intuition and feeling as well as logic and reasoning — can involve, for example, the use of pictures, modelling, drama, mime, dance, and so on. Also, all sorts of simple discussion exercises can be devised to promote reflective and intuitive, as distinct from intellectual and cerebral, exploration of symbolic meanings.[13]

4) Teaching pupils to study simple objects very, very closely — flowers, stones, fruit, candles, all sorts of ikons and images. The goal of such attention, to evoke an incredibly high standard, is the state of mind and being commended by Rainer Maria Rilke in a comment he once made on a still life by Cezanne: Cezanne did not paint 'I like it', he said, but 'There it is.'[14]

5) Using autobiography and journalling techniques; in this respect teachers of religious education have much to learn not only from the field of spiritual direction[15] but also from the best practice to be found amongst their colleagues who teach 'English' — all pupils have stories to tell, masses and masses of stories, and all teachers, ideally, need expertise and talent in helping these to be released, and brought to birth.

6) Ensuring that inservice courses for teachers use a wide variety of stimuli and techniques, of the kinds listed above, and help to put teachers in touch with their own stories, in particular their own childhoods and growings-up. As a teacher you need to know and befriend the child within yourself before you can realistically and objectively know and befriend, and welcome and care about, the children in your classroom.[16]

These extremely brief notes begin to sketch what religious education could look like, or begin to look like, both in classrooms and in teacher training, when the model of teacher as spiritual director is explored in practice. What are the main objections, though, to this model, and how may the objections be answered, both in theory and in pedagogical practice?

One set of objections will come from the mass media, insofar as they see profit in running stories that such teaching is untraditional, un-Christian, un-English, and unlikely to lead to high examination passes in the national curriculum. To reply to this kind of objection we need not only sound political and public relations skills, but also intellectual confidence to describe and defend spiritual direction from a grounding in entirely mainstream (though neglected) traditions of prayer and contemplation, and from within the framework of much modern and secular science and medicine.[17]

Another kind of objection is that the vast majority of the conventions, routines and procedures of everyday school life and classroom teaching are inimical to a concern for spirituality: 'How do you assess your pupils' spiritual development?' — 'Oh, out of 20 usually.' This objection is valid, of course, but should renew our determination to change the routines and conventions. The micro- political task of engaging in such change is a major aspect, arguably, of the practical work required of every teacher of religious education. Together with teaching itself, such work constitutes the attachment and caring pole of our lives.

A third set of objections may of course come from faith communities — is not spiritual direction, they may reasonably ask, and teaching people how to pray and to meditate, their own distinctive responsibility, not the responsibility of mainstream county schools? This is certainly an important and serious objection and cannot be handled as cavalierly as the first two objections. It would be better dealt with in dialogue and reflection about real practice and real practical possibilities rather than in a speculative think-piece such as this, and in one-sided words on a printed page. Suffice to repeat the claim being made here: that spiritual development is not only distinct from moral development but is also distinct, in certain very significant respects, from initiation into, and nurturing in, any one religious tradition. In such real dialogue and reflection it would be useful to have in mind that famous and beautiful meditation of Rabindranath Tagore about children on the seashore:

> *They build their houses with sand*
> *and they play with empty shells.*

> *With withered leaves they weave their boats*
> *and smiling float them on the vast deep*

> *Children have their play*
> *on the seashore of worlds.*

Tagore goes on to contrast the children on the shore with fisher-people, sailors, explorers, merchants, out there beyond the horizon, and he notes their innocent 'uncaring', their unawareness of danger and menace, and of death by drowning. Watching their passionate playfulness he sees an image of all humankind — their playing and meeting is like that of adult religion and culture against the backdrop of immensity and mortality. The skies and the ocean are then unboundedly gentle and loving as well as unboundedly perilous: 'death-dealing waves sing meaningless ballads to the children, even like a mother while rocking her baby's cradle.' Let us go out into our classrooms and our schools, and into the micropolitics of turning them round into good places for humans to be, and out into wider society and the political tasks of building and defending new structures of power between individuals and groupings, Tagore is in effect saying, with hopeful confidence in ourselves and each other. With faith that all shall be well, that all manner of thing shall be well. Trusting in the insights and enlightenments of our respective spiritual traditions, and in our own creativity and playfulness. And in the worthwhileness of political endeavour. And caring and not caring:

> *On the seashore of endless worlds*
> *children meet;*

> *Tempest roams in the pathless sky,*
> *ships get wrecked in the trackless water,*
> *death is abroad, and children play;*

> *On the seashore of endless worlds*
> *is the great meeting of children.*

PART FOUR:
POLICIES AND
PROGRAMMES OF
CHANGE

14. You Haven't Lost Yet, Kids
—an address to headteachers

Speaking to captive audiences is particularly hazardous. If, as on this occasion, people are present through a three-line whip brandished by local politicians and education officers, there is the danger of adding insult to injury: of either boring the audience with platitudes or else of offending them with abrasiveness or jokiness. If, alternatively, the audience is hugely expectant, there is the danger of not being able to catch and articulate for them what it is they most want to be said, and thus of letting them down. If, however, the hazards of boring, offending or disappointing are avoided, then there are moral dangers to, so to speak, one's own soul and salvation: dangers of taking self-absorbed pride in one's own handling of language and of the social situation, and of drawing irresponsible private pleasure from living dangerously, and from surviving.

The audience on this occasion consisted of about 200 people — all the headteachers in one particular LEA in the West Midlands, plus all the local advisory service, some college lecturers, and some members of support services. What tone of voice and general posture was it appropriate to adopt, what shared feelings and experience should be implied, what degree of gravity should be expressed towards the occasion itself? These were some of the inevitable questions in the background.

* * * * *

I have journeyed to Walsall only once before today. It was on a Saturday in April this year, and the venture was in connection with the fact that my teenage son and I are faithful, indeed I confess fanatical, supporters of Oxford United Football Club. There was this crucial promotion battle, towards the end of last season, with your local team.

We parked our car some distance from the ground, put on our scarves, buttoned up our collars so that we could pass incognito amongst people whose loyalties and affiliations were no doubt different from our own, and started off walking. We came in due course to a canal, and we paused on the bridge and looked down at the water. Inveterate educator and tiresome parent that I am, I began giving my son a brief overview of the industrial revolution and of capitalism, the development of the iron heart of England, the migrations of labour which took place in the course of the nineteenth century, the interconnection between urbanisation at home and imperialism overseas, the nature of exploitation everywhere; and I reminded him that his mother and I, recently researching the family history, had established that several of his great-great-great grandparents had sold their labour to workshops and foundries in this area in the early nineteenth century — in Bloxwich, Willenhall, Blakenall, Cannock, Cradley Heath, Dudley.

I became aware that Ben was not paying entirely rapt attention and looked up from the canal to ascertain the reason. It was twofold. For one thing his collar had come undone and his affiliation was showing. For the other, a group of Walsall supporters was bearing down on us. I began to visualise the coverage which the impending episode would have in Monday's *Oxford Mail*, and I wondered whether we might be so fortunate and honoured as to appear not only on a news page but in the obituary columns also. The Walsall supporters came up to us, looked at Ben's scarf, then down at the canal at which they had seen us gazing, then back at us. 'No need to commit suicide,' one of them said, 'you haven't lost yet, kids'. And they went on their way, chuckling at their own wit, and taking manifest pride in their own tolerance and magnanimity.

Now it may be, Mr Chairman, that there are one or two people in the audience here this morning who are wondering whether this episode is really and truly relevant to the subject-matter of today's conference. Which is, perhaps I would do well at this stage to recall, multicultural

151

education. Anyone who does have wonderings along these lines may go on to conjecture that the reason I have started with an irrelevant and time-wasting story is that I am feeling ill-at-ease. Such a conjecture, Mr Chairman, would be (it says here) correct: indeed, I am feeling ill-at-ease.

There are many reasons for this discomfort. First, I am an outsider here — an insensitive bull in the china shop of local politics and local intrigues. Second, the subject of today's conference is deeply controversial and emotive, and I am bound therefore to irritate, to give offence, to alienate. Third, there may already be people here who would rather be somewhere else. Fourth, I belong to a species — local education authority adviser — whose existence most people here, since they are headteachers, no doubt hold to be entirely unnecessary. Fifth, this conference is a major event, and I cannot possibly justify the honour you have paid me in inviting me to speak at its start. Sixth, the location where I usually work, Berkshire, is almost certainly pictured by most people here as a rural, soft, sleepy, languid, la-dee-da sort of place, where no-one could possibly acquire experience relevant to real life, for example life in the West Midlands. And seventh, both lecturing and listening to lectures are so often — on this subject, incidentally, more than on most — merely draining and demoralising.

Yes, there are many reasons, Mr Chairman, why I am feeling ill-at-ease, many reasons for starting with an irrelevant and time-wasting story.

Mind you, the story wasn't one hundred per cent irrelevant. For after all it touched on the history of industrialism and capitalism in this country, and on capitalism's thirst for migrations of labour; it touched on loyalties and affiliations, and on prejudices, tribalisms and fear; it touched on relations between parent and child, and on identities and roots in time and space. So not totally irrelevant, in its content, to a lecture on multicultural education. Nor entirely irrelevant in its form. For it used overblown, melodramatic language to describe — well, truly, to distort — a trivial episode; and in reminding us thus of the great chasm which can gape between language and action, rhetoric and reality, it was by no means irrelevant to a lecture and to a conference which amongst other things are going to be about the uses, and the misuses, and the non-uses, of formal policy statements.

Be that as it may, we continue with a story which is more obviously relevant. Shortly after I had started my current work, I was visiting a school in Berkshire and talking with the headteacher. 'So,' he said, 'you'd like me to introduce multicultural education?' — 'Yes,' I said, 'please.' — 'Well certainly I can introduce multicultural education for you, I can introduce anything. I introduced integrated humanities, I introduced computers, I introduced school-industry links, oh I know how to introduce things, I know how to get things done. There's a very good programme on television, you know, for headteachers — it's on every week, and it shows you exactly how to get things done if you're a headteacher. I don't know whether you've ever seen it, it's called Dallas, and really it's very good, but anyway, about multicultural education, yes I'll introduce it, no problem.'

He looked me in the eye. 'Well actually,' he said, 'there's one problem.' Pause. 'The difference between multicultural education and all the other things I've introduced is that nobody knows, and nobody will ever know, what multicultural education actually is.' And he looked at me with that air which headteachers no doubt adopt everywhere when they know that they have just won point, game, set, match and tournament against an adviser. I said nothing — for after all it was getting late, and I needed to be on my way — but I did think to myself that one day I would be able to re-tell this story to make a point. Today's the day.

The point is that whilst most certainly multicultural education *can* be defined, the theoretical task of defining it cannot be dissociated, if you are a headteacher, from practical management tasks, techniques, strategies and processes. The vast majority of books and documents on multicultural education completely ignore this fundamental fact of life. They go on at tedious and demoralising length about various ideals, but seldom if ever recall and consider the complexities of organisational life, and the complex juggling and footwork skills which are required, day-by-day and minute-by-minute, of every headteacher.

For example, treatises on multicultural education totally ignore that whole body of headteacher-friendly management maxims customarily known as Sod's Law. You know the sort of thing: 'It's impossible to make a plan foolproof, because fools are so ingenious' ; 'If things appear to be getting better, it's because you've overlooked something' ; 'If you explain everything so absolutely clearly that no-one can possibly misunderstand, somebody will'; 'Any project in a school which depends on people being reliable is unreliable'; 'When in doubt, tell the truth — unless, that is, you are an unusually skilful liar'; 'If those around suddenly start smiling when things are going wrong it's because they have just realised that they can blame the whole wretched disaster on you'; 'Advisers and inspectors do sometimes stumble on the truth, but always pick themselves up and carry on regardless'; 'Even probationary teachers are not infallible'; 'School governors do sometimes behave intelligently and rationally, but only after all other possibilities have been thoroughly researched and exhausted'; 'There are three key stages in local government decision-making: stage one, get ready: stage two, fire: stage three, take aim'; 'Always remember, as a headteacher, that you shouldn't believe in miracles — you should rely on them'.

Not that those are the only maxims which headteachers use. Also there is more hopeful and more generous lore amongst headteachers.[1] I should like to recall here eight simple but fundamental things which all headteachers know about good management, and relate each to the field of multicultural education. Then I shall respond very directly to that headteacher whom I mentioned earlier, the one who commended Dallas, by defining — well, more accurately, by discussing competing definitions of — multicultural education.

First, it is essential, if a project or development in a school is to be successful, that the head should very clearly be seen to be in favour of it. At the very least this means checking up on it, showing an interest in it, turning up at meetings about it, speaking and writing in public about it, and so on. Headteachers' views are deafeningly stated, sometimes, not through what they do say but through what they don't — through, that is, their silences and absences. With a subject such as multicultural education it's important, further, that heads should be clearly seen to be standing on the line, to be taking sides and therefore risks.

But whilst the actions and non-actions of headteachers are fundamental in any change process in a school, heads are not (contrary to the assumptions of some children, many parents and most staff) actually omnipotent. Other factors are of course crucially important too, for example the other seven points in this list of eight.

Second, it is essential that staff should feel that they own any new project. Amongst other things this means that there has to be a lot of patient and frank deliberation, and a culture in the staffroom which encourages and sustains such deliberation. People need to be able to think aloud, and to muse and speculate. They will not do this if they are scared at every moment of being labelled and criticised by colleagues who believe themselves to be more aware, enlightened, committed or reconstructed. One of a headteacher's most important leadership tasks is that of helping the staff to build and defend a culture of trust and openness, and of vigorous and rigorous debate, amongst themselves.[2]

Third, commitment often or usually occurs, if it does occur, through taking part in argument and advocacy, and pressurising and campaigning. It follows that staff need not only certain knowledge but also certain skills and qualities. For example, they need negotiating and advocacy skills, in order to be able to deal with sceptical colleagues and with (yes) sceptical and feet-dragging headteachers. And they need qualities of perseverance and courage. They will not otherwise be able to handle failure and defeat, nor mistrust and suspicion from the very people whom they are intending to help.

Fourth, it is important to note and to document progress and successes. In the field of multicultural education this is often psychologically very difficult, for much of the progress we make is paltry and derisory in relation to the magnitude of the task before us. Nevertheless we may and we should take legitimate pride in whatever is achieved, for otherwise we may not have the strength to persevere when things go wrong.

Fifth, it follows, there must be an expectation of errors and alleged errors, and of actual or imagined failures, and of threat and pain and stress. The management task is not to shield staff from pain and stress, but to provide and protect space in which staff can face such pain and stress, and cope productively with them. This involves, and depends on, communicating care and respect, and trust and confidence. If and when people feel that they are receiving fundamental care and respect from others, they can cope with quite high levels of anxiety and discomfort. This is a challenging point not only for the managers of schools, incidentally, but also for the organisers of conferences, and for lecturers at conferences.[3]

TABLE 4: CONTROVERSIES IN RACE AND EDUCATION — THREE PERSPECTIVES

A — 'conforming'	B — 'reforming'	C — 'transforming'
Immigrants came to Britain in the 1950's and 1960s because the laws on immigration were not strict enough.	Ethnic minorities came to Britain because they has a right to and because they wanted a better life.	Black people came to Britain, as to other countries, because their labour was required by the economy.
Immigrants should integrate as quickly as possible with the British way of life.	Ethnic minorities should be able to maintain their language and cultural heritage.	Black people have to defend themselves against racist laws and practices, and to struggle for racial justice.
There is some racial prejudice in Britain but it's only human nature, and Britain is a much more tolerant place than most other countries.	There are some misguided individuals and extremist groups in Britain, but basically our society is just and democratic, and provides equality.	Britain is a racist society, and has been for several centuries. Racism is to do with power structures more than with the attitudes of individuals.
It is counter-productive to try to remove prejudice — you can't force people to like each other by bringing in laws and regulations.	Prejudice is based on ignorance and misunderstandings. It can be removed by personal contacts and the provision of information.	'Prejudice' is caused by, it is not the cause of, unjust structures and procedures. It can be removed only by dismantling these.
There should be provision of English as a Second Language in schools, but otherwise 'children are all children, we should treat all children exactly the same' — it is wrong to notice or emphasize cultural or racial differences. Low achievement in immigrant pupils is caused by factors within immigrant families and cultures.	Schools should recognize and affirm ethnic minority children's background, culture and language... celebrate festivals, organise international evenings, use and teach mother tongues, community languages, teach about ethnic minority history, art, music, religion, literature.	Priorities in education are for there to be more black people in positions of power and influence — as heads, senior teachers, governors, education officers, elected members; and to remove discrimination in the curriculum, classroom methods and school organisation: and to teach directly about equality and justice and against racism.

Sixth, very obviously, there must be sufficient resources — money and the things which money can buy. These are vitally important not only in themselves but also as symbols — they reflect a school's priorities and commitments. The country is, alas, getting littered during the 1980s with policy statements on multicultural edcuation which are accompanied with totally inadequate resources, or with no resources at all.

Seventh, another very obvious point : there must be clarity about who is going to do what by when. Clear terms of reference, strict instructions, precise target dates and deadlines - everyone here today knows how very important such things are. We know also, in our heart of hearts, that multicultural education is a field in which such elementary reqirements are more often honoured in the breach than in the observance.

Eighth, we need to be clear that the main reason why human beings ever change what they are doing is that they perceive it to be in their own best interests to change, or else against their own interests not to change. In other words, when they are reaching for carrots or else shrinking from sticks. Too often multicultural education is seen as an optional extra, something 'moral' and altruistic to take on if and when, but only if and when, more pressing things have been seen to first. A lot of hard thought has got to be given, however, by headteachers and also by many others, to the central importance of material interests and selfish (but legitimate) motivations. The issues here are not easy, either philosophically or pragmatically, but we should avoid the temptation, and force one another to avoid the temptation, to ignore them.

If there is going to be debate and deliberation about multicultural education, it is useful to have in one's mind an overall map of the views that are likely to be expressed. One kind of customary map in this area involves distinguishing between three main perspectives, and to refer to them respectively as the assimilation perspective, the cultural diversity perspective and the race equality perspective. They are summarised in one of the handouts provided as resource material at today's conference. I am going to refer to them simply with three letters — respectively the A perspective, the B and the C.[4]

Each of the three perspectives can be summarised with a golden rule. The golden rule for the first is 'when in Rome do as the Romans do', or alternatively 'immigration is the sincerest form of flattery'. It envisages that an essential race relations priority is to make ethnic minority people, including in particular their children and grandchildren in schools, as 'British' as possible. The golden rule summarising the second perspective goes something like 'variety is the spice of life'. Its recurring discourse is to do with culture, ethnicity, diversity, pluralism. The golden rule summarising the third perspective is 'them who's got the gold makes the rules'. Essential key concepts in the third perspective, in other words, are power, wealth, decision-making, politics and economics. The third perspective places 'multicultural education' (inverted commas now because the term has different connotations here) within the context of the history of industrialism and capitalism, and of migrations of labour. It is based on a structural, not individualistic, theory of racism.[5]

I am particularly interested this morning in the distinction and choice between the second perspective and the third. They can be highlighted with reference to a passage in one of the conference papers. In this paper a headteacher provides a very readable and warm account of multicultural, multi-ethnic education in a London primary school. He describes ways in which the school welcomes and affirms children's varying cultural backgrounds through the use of appropriate books and artefacts, the celebration of festivals, food evenings, the involvement of parents, visits to the Commonwealth Institute, and so on. It is clear that the head and staff are aware that prejudices and stereotypes exist within themselves as well as within the world at large and are prepared to examine and to change their own attitudes. At one stage in the paper he writes this:

> It would be quite wrong to pretend that it has all been easy. Changing attitudes, especially one's own, is never that. I still shudder at the memory of the time, shortly after I joined the school, when I was interviewing a disappointed Black mother about secondary transfer. 'Never mind,' I heard myself saying, 'we mustn't look on the black side of things!'

Now it is laudable that the head was monitoring his own language self-critically, and that he 'heard himself' saying something. It is laudable too that he writes with frankness about a mistake which he made — such frankness is likely to stimulate similar openness and honesty in others. Further it is laudable that he is critical and ashamed of his use of the word black. But I hope it is not merely churlish, and not merely a case of more-anti-racist-than-thou, to note certain ironies in this brief story of which the headteacher himself seems unaware. These ironies clarify the distinction between perspective B and perspective C, and show that he himself holds perspective B.

The conversation is about transfer to secondary school. The mother is worried about the proposed placement because she believes that it will damage her child's life-chances, for she has reason to believe that resources and opportunities at the one school are superior to those at the other. Multicultural education has failed to give her child what she most desires — the best possible life-chances. The headteacher 'interviewing' her seems more concerned by the tactlessness of his remark than about the personal racism it may reflect, and more concerned to reconcile her to her station in life than to try to see education and society from her point of view.

Elsewhere in the conference papers is a further interesting example of the distinction between the two perspectives and of the ways in which we white people are often apparently unaware of our own motives. A headteacher writes that 'all along we have felt the absence of authority figures of different ethnic origins in the school. . . ' At first hearing it sounds as if the head is more concerned with life-chances than with life-style — he is keen, it sounds, to raise the achievement of black students through providing positive role-models for them. But the passage continues:

> We have gone some way to remedying this by having a steel band tutor, and through the P.E. inspectorate a tutor for sport.

This extraordinary emphasis on relative trivialities invites us to re-read the previous sentence, and to hear a rather more sinister meaning. 'We need more *authority* figures,' the head is now heard saying. It sounds as if his motive for having black teachers is to exercise greater social control. And indeed it often seems to happen that the principal purpose for multicultural education is precisely this, the social control of black youth. For example, the formal report to Walsall Education Committee which has been sent to all of us in connection with today's conference implies that one major reason for promoting multiculturalism is to avoid riots in the streets. The same report uses the words 'culture', 'cultural' or 'ethnic' 37 times, but the word 'discrimination' only twice, 'justice' only once, and 'racism' not at all.

I ought at this stage to clarify where I think I stand in relation to the three perspectives — and clarify too who I think I'm talking to! I see myself as holding the third perspective, C, and a close study of the conference papers leads me to see this conference as an attempt by the organisers to persuade headteachers to move from perspective A to perspective B. I do not make this observation in order to criticise but for the sake of honesty, and to explain why I have adopted, and am adopting, the particular style and register of language and lecturing which you are witnessing. The lecture would be very different, particularly from now on, if I perceived this audience as being made up wholly or mainly of people who hold persepective C.

There are five brief points which I should like to mention and emphasise with regard to perspective C. The first is that few if any people are ever converted to it through listening to a lecture advocating it : which is by way of saying, you may be relieved to hear, that it is not going to be explicitly advocated here.

Second, it is the case that most people who hold this third perspective have come to it through, or via, the second perspective. For this reason if for no other (though there are in fact other good reasons) they should be tolerant and friendly towards perspective B, not merely critical and dismissive, delighting in their own, as they suppose, greater enlightenment. (I wonder, in this connection, whether I myself seemed tolerant and friendly, or on the contrary unfairly critical, in my remarks just now about the headteachers quoted in the conference papers?)

A third point is that whilst most people seem to come to perspective C, if they come to it at all, by way of perspective B, there are definitely other routes. In particular it is very relevant to note that feminists (including male feminists, of course) often have an immediate and intuitive insight into this third cluster of views on race equality. In both fields — gender equality and race equality — the key terms and concepts have very similar meanings: direct and indirect discrimination, for example, also positive action, participation in decision-making, mobilisation, solidarity, consciousness-rasing, structural change, justice.

A fourth point is to do with the interaction and interface between perspective C and socialism. Is this third perspective inherently marxist and revolutionary, as certain right-wing critics are maintaining? If so, what are the implications of this for everyday practical politics, given that the vast majority of people in the country, including the vast majority of teachers and headteachers, and the vast majority of black people, are not marxists, and do not recognise marxist socialism as charting a realistic or desirable future for them?[6] These are extremely important questions, but are unlikely to be quite so fascinating to this morning's audience, I daresay, as they are within the enclaves of perspective C. I will say no more on this topic, except that I know of no evidence to suggest that a socialist society would necessarily be less racist than a capitalist one, and that I think there are valuable things which can be done for race equality under capitalism, and by faithful members of the Conservative Party. (Am I myself, by the way, a socialist? This is a question which one or two people here may be wondering. One answer to this question, Mr Chairman, is good gracious no, of course I'm not a socialist, how could I be, I'm a local government officer. That answer would be both ironic and evasive. Both irony and evasiveness are occasionally defensible. Particularly, I humbly submit, at moments such as the present one.)

Fifth, it is important to recognise that perspective C frequently has difficulty in talking about certain matters which are of central importance in perspective B, and that this is very unfortunate. For example and in particular, it often has an impoverished vocabulary for talking about religious faith and identity, and about inter faith dialogue and learning. Many black people in this country are devoutly religious, but they find very little affirmation and understanding of their faith amongst white anti-racists.[7] Also, it is relevant to comment here on the third perspective's use of the word 'black'. The term is valuable in emphasising, insofar as it does indeed emphasise, that the fundamental reality to be named is racism — 'black' people are all those who are victims of racism. The single term obscures, however, the fact that racism acts in significantly different ways on different communities, and on different ethnic, cultural and religious groups; and that large numbers of people in Britain from Bangladesh, India and Pakistan do not at present, and quite possibly never will, define themselves politically as black. [8]

As this lecture draws towards a close, I should like to touch on some practicalities — practical priorities which can be embarked on pending, so to speak, one's choices and decisions between perspective B and perspective C. I shall speak here to four headings: language awareness; policy statements; monitoring; and participation in decision-making.

Regarding language awareness, I recall a letter I received recently from a headteacher requesting extra staffing to assist with English as a Second Language. He enclosed notes from some of his staff giving a detailed explanation of the 'problem' — the problem, they said, was that large numbers of children only spoke pidgin English. They spelt the word pidgin in a way which implied that their point of comparison was a parrot or budgerigar rather than, shall we say, the dialect spoken by BBC news readers. Now maybe those teachers did need extra staffing at their school, extra colleagues to provide organisational space and slack. But what primarily they needed was far more awareness of what language is, what English is, what the relationship is between standard and non-standard forms of a language, and of how oral and written language develop.[9]

A classroom in which there is lively interest in linguistic diversity, both between languages and amongst registers and repertoires of English, is one in which bilingual and potentially bilingual children will prosper most readily, and in which — incidentally — all children are likely to prosper. Terms such as language awareness, language studies, linguistic diversity, and so on, evoke a field of activity in which teachers of all age-groups and attainment-levels can engage tomorrow, or anyway no later than next Monday morning. There's no need to wait until you have sorted out the theoretical differences between, for example, multiculturalism and anti-racism.

With regard to formal policy statements, I note and commend one of the papers provided for today's conference by the head of a Walsall school. He makes three vitally important points. First, he emphasises that a school staff needs to have a discussion of fundamental principles and to agree on basic terminology. 'Without some discussion of principles,' he writes, 'it is unlikely that staff attitudes will be receptive to change, or that awareness will be increased, or that there will be a clear idea of what commitment the school might make.' Second, he emphasises the importance of involving parents in the policy-making process. Third, most importantly of all, he shows that a school policy must be sufficiently detailed, and sufficiently well phrased and drafted, for it to serve as an instrument for monitoring and evaluation.[10]

On this question of monitoring I recall a meeting which I attended recently between some headteachers and black community leaders. 'We agree,' the heads said, though only after a lot of discussion, 'that we ought to monitor what is happening to black children so far as their academic progress is concerned.' They agreed further that they would start with maths. 'Good,' said the community leaders, ' and we want you also to monitor the distribution of your own resources. We are aware from various newspaper articles that not all teachers of maths do in fact have qualifications in this subject. We want to know not only how our children are doing in maths exams and tests, but also how qualified in maths the teachers are, in the schools and classes where our children happen to be.' A vital distinction was being drawn between the distribution of rewards and the distribution of resources. Both kinds of distribution need constant and vigilant monitoring.

With regard to participation in decision-making, the essential point follows readily and directly from that story about the meeting between headteachers and community leaders: we have got to involve black people in all our deliberations and decisions. One reason for this is that we white people cannot be trusted — we cannot trust ourselves and each other, let alone expect black people to trust us, to be adequately vigilant and self-critical. We do not know where the shoe pinches : we do not know what it is like to be black in a white society. We can never adequately know even the bare minimum we need to know in order to take our part in building race equality. That is a pragmatic reason for involving black people — we should involve them because it's useful and necessary. Also we should involve them because it is right. We must make real in our journey the destination which we seek: adapting Mahatma Gandhi slightly, we must see that 'there is no way to equality — for equality is the way.'

A word of conclusion. When you are a young teacher you dream of what you'll one day do as a headteacher, to shape and change the world. If you were a young teacher in the 1960s, as I was, one of the writers who moved you was John Holt. In particular there was that great essay of his entitled 'Schools are Bad Places for Kids'. [11] Many years later, now that you are a headteacher, you find that you are not changing the world either quickly enough or deeply enough. In particular you are likely to be disappointed if your ideal is to build equality and justice in and through education.

You are overwhelmed by requests, demands, expectations, pressures. There's that mountain of things to have been done, but in fact not done, by yesterday. There are all those unbearable letters, circulars and memos thudding each week onto your desk from the education office. The unions. The parents. Children, and the childishness of adults. The insensitivity of the government. You could scream. Everyone seems to think that it's impossible to disappoint you, to hurt you, to overwork you, to break you; that you know everything, and can perform or prevent anything; that you alone, in all the world, do not know the meaning of phrases such as 'the last straw' and 'people poisoning'.[12] You realise there's an article which John Holt didn't write — 'Schools are Bad Places for Headteachers'.

And yet! You are in a good place. Not the only good place on earth, but certainly in one good place, and your life and work can be very worthwhile. How shall I now say good-bye to you? One way would be with the words with which some of your fellow citizens once greeted my son and myself: you haven't lost yet, kids. But I will in fact close with some rather stronger good-byes, three of them altogther. One is contemporary. One is continental. One is ancient. Ladies and gentlemen the headteachers of Walsall, take care; *courage;* fare ye very well.

15. Worth the Paper it's Written On?
— the making and use of policy

Two of the essays in this book — this one and the one entitled Believing Enough? *— have their origins very specifically in work and experience in the County of Berkshire, 1979-1985. In that period a policy statement on education for racial equality was slowly developed, and eventually published and promulgated; then in due course it was supported — though rather quirkily and jerkily — through the creation and filling of a number of new posts. The policy became well known nationally as well as within Berkshire — it was quoted in full in the Swann Report,* Education for All, *and the preliminary discussion paper on which it was based,* Education for Equality, *was reprinted and nationally circulated by the Inner London Education Authority. Many other LEAs around the country, and also many individual institutions, adopted it or adapted it for themselves. Its national influence and significance were noted, and bitterly deplored, by journals and pamphlets of the New Right.*

At the time that the policy was developed and first published Berkshire County Council was 'hung', with no single political party having an outright majority on the Education Committee. Later in the decade the Conservative Party had a large majority, and the first thing it did on taking power was to change the basic terms of political and educational debate: it abolished the phrase 'education for racial equality' as the essential conceptualisation to guide policy in this field, and replaced it with the term 'multi-cultural education.' 'This change of name was significant,' explained a senior politician later. 'The old name suggested an aggressive propaganda campaign designed to brainwash people into changing their thinking. It assumed that Berkshire people are naturally racist and antagonistic towards ethnic minorities, and that it is part of the job of education to convert them away from this.'

Next, the new ruling group attempted to abrogate the formal policy on race equality, and to replace it with a grotesque document stressing integration and assimilation. ('Britain needs to maintain its individuality, culture and heritage... Our textbooks and displays, the general ethos of our schools and colleges, all that we do, should reflect a reasonable pride in our nation and things British.') If this attempt had been successful, it would have been a resounding victory for the New Right nationally, and for 'anti-anti-racism' throughout the country. By the same token it would have been a major setback for race equality in education, nationally as well as locally, and it would have helped to consolidate the more illiberal and narrowly chauvinist aspects of the Education Reform Act.

There was a massive campaign to maintain the Berkshire policy, however, and this campaign was successful. It involved the submission of over 700 letters; several petitions, deputations, marches and demonstrations; two vigils; a remarkable mobilisation of church organisations and of mosques, temples, synagogues and gurdwaras; a great deal of skilfully orchestrated correspondence and coverage in the local press and in certain sections of the national press; and great energy on the part of many members of the education service. The ruling political group had no option but to retreat in ignominy. The episode was a resounding defeat not only for them but also for the New Right nationally.

Whether the policy statement is actually having a deep and lasting effect on the creation of equality and justice in Berkshire, however, is another matter and will have to await the verdict of history. In the meanwhile this essay, originally presented to a conference at the University of London shortly after the policy statement had been formally published, discusses the nature and possible uses of written policy statements, and the factors likely to affect whether they are in practice of any real value.

Every LEA, it is said, should have one: a policy statement on anti-racist and multicultural education. Yes, but why ? And how? And what should the statement actually state? And to what literary genre do such statements belong? — In what ways are they distinctively different from other kinds of statement, for example from sonnets, love letters, prayers or undergraduate essays? Or , more seriously, from edicts and laws, rules and requirements?

These are the questions to be considered here. Underlying them is a further question. It does not at first sight, admittedly, seem to be worth asking, for surely everyone already knows the answer. The further question is this: what is a local education authority ? The question is not quite so stupid as it may seem. People have a variety of mental models of LEAs — just as, more obviously, they have a variety of metaphors and abuse to describe the one with which they are most familiar. (Similarly there are distinctive terms to describe county halls and town halls — at least one grand headquarters in the shires is known by local teachers as Buggers' Palace, and at least one office in London as Kafka House.) There is no great point in trying to clarify what an LEA policy statement is, and what it is not, and how it should appropriately be developed, and so on, unless one first tries to clarify what kind of a beast an LEA basically is. What is it, in terms of organisation theory ? What are its distinctive tasks and functions? What, behind the pious rhetoric which all LEAs use in their mission statements about 'providing a service' and 'responding to the needs of the community', et cetera and et cetera, is actually going on?

One approach to trying to understand LEAs, as also many other kinds of organisation, involves using what has come to be known as systems thinking.[1] The basic structure of an LEA can be visualised with a well-known diagram such as this:

$$\text{INPUTS} \Rightarrow \text{LEA} \Rightarrow \text{OUTPUTS}$$

The essential or primary task of an LEA, according to such a model, is to take resources from its environment, process or transmute them in some way, and then export them back to the environment. LEAs are thus like living organisms which take in energy of various kinds and use it to affect or shape their surroundings in such a way as to ensure a continual life-giving supply of the energy which they need. And they are like commercial enterprises, which take in raw materials; process and sell them; and then use some of the proceeds to secure further raw materials.

The primary raw material taken in by an LEA is money — partly from central government, partly from the poll tax. The primary output is also money: an LEA is a complex organisation whose purpose in life is to transform money into money. The essential questions are not — *pace* the Education Reform Act and the New Right — about efficiency, effectiveness and economy, but about equality and equity. Who benefits, the question is, from these operations? What, for example, is the text which encodes everything ? Is it from the first chapter of the gospel according to Saint Luke, verse 51: 'put down the mighty from their seat... filled the hungry with good things... the rich sent empty away'? Or is it from the twenty-fifth chapter of the gospel according to Saint Matthew, verse 29: 'unto everyone that hath shall be given, and he shall have abundance: but from him that hath not shall be taken away even that which he hath'? In other words, the question about the flow of resources through an LEA is this: does the flow reflect and reinforce, or does it challenge and change, structures and patterns of exploitation and inequality in wider society? [2]

The overall pattern of the the flow of resouces can be pictured in a simple circular diagram. (see page 169)

A systems model such as this has three main advantages in the present context. First, it implies and invites a re-conceptualisation of the conventional concept of racial discrimination. Conventionally, discrimination is seen as occurring in inter-personal or small-scale encounters between the providers of services and resources (including jobs) on the one hand and clients or potential clients on the other. Now certainly such discrimination is very serious, and needs to be strenuously identified and removed. But the advantage of a systems model is that it focuses on equity in the overall distribution of resources, not just (so to speak) on individual episodes. To what extent do black people and white benefit differentially from expenditure on, for example, sixth form education? On mandatory and discretionary grants for higher and further education? On Youth and Community services? On an LEA's instrumental music service? On expensive laboratory equipment and information technology? On grants for the inservice training and professional development of teachers? Analogous questions to these can

Figure 6: ASPECTS OF LEA POLICY

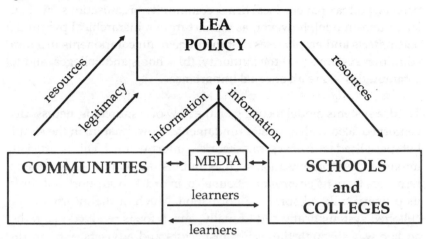

Figure 6 recalls that:
(i) an LEA has three main kinds of input — resources, legitimacy and information;
(ii) an LEA policy, accordingly, is a mental and organisational framework for allocating resources, securing legitimacy and evaluating information;
(iii) learners are continually moving backwards and forwards between institutions and communities;
(iv) the local media are an important two way channel of information;
(v) a key question is who benefits — who, in which communities, gets what?

also of course be asked about the distribution of scarce resources within individual schools.

A second advantage of a systems model is that it emphasises that all people in an LEA have an important part to play in the overall change process. Too many of our conventional assumptions about educational management involve a top-down, hierarchical model, a pyramid. At the peak of the pyramid, it is envisaged, is the Education Committee, making policy and taking policy decisions. Then just below the Committee but above everyone else, is the Director of Education and the Director's senior management team. Then beneath that group are head-teachers, and deputy heads, and teachers with incentive allowances from E down to A. Then MPG. Beneath the most junior teachers there are the pupils, similarly arranged in hierarchies, layers and ranks of various kinds involving the use of terms such as senior, middle, junior, top, high, low, etc, and reflecting back to teachers and administrators through this stratification the essential and abiding nature of all reality.

Somewhere outside the pyramid, in this conventional picture, there are parents, poll tax payers, local firms, community organisations. A circular systems model, however, as distinct from a hierarchical pyramidal one, reflects and emphasises that the three main components in a local education system — (a) the authority, (b) schools and colleges, and (c) communities — are all of equal importance.

Third, a systems model focusing on the flow of resources is, necessarily, concerned also with a further fundamental flow: that of, in the simple but specialised term of systems theorists, information.[3] This is crucially important. An organisation such as an LEA takes in not only material resources from its environment but also, in order to support and direct its primary task, all sorts of information. Much of the information is collected systematically and formally; much too is received in a rather ad hoc way through the use of inspectors and advisers, who in this connection are often known, significantly, as an authority's eyes and ears; and a very great deal comes in unsolicited, in the form of requests, demands, campaigns and pressures, and coverage in the local press. Either way — whether collected more or less systematically or whether only received — information has to be processed: the organisation has to make sense of it. If you want to study an LEA as a complex organisation, it follows, you have to do two main things: (a) study the mechanisms which it uses to distribute resources; and (b) study the processes by which it makes sense of information.

This brief reminder of systems theory is almost, for our present purposes, complete. But there is one more important preliminary point to do with the nature of resources. The assumption so far here has been that the only significant kind of resource is money and what money can buy. But also there is the resource known as legitimacy. (The semantic equation being assumed here is Wealth plus Legitimacy equals Power.) Now certainly legitimacy is related to the control and possession of money, but it is separable for the sake of analysis. It comes most dramatically and critically into an LEA every four years, in the form of votes. It comes also— or fails to come — daily, to officers as well as to politicians, through letters, papers, conversations, personal contacts. An observant and cynical visitor to an education office would conclude, if they had the opportunity to sit in on the countless informal and semiformal meetings amongst officers which take place every day, that an inordinate amount of time and energy is devoted to, as the term is,

'maintaining credibility': demonstrating to headteachers and governing bodies and to the general public that you're in control and know
what you're doing, or concealing from them the fearful reality that
you're not and you don't.

In addition to receiving legitimacy, LEAs are also providers of it. Most
obviously, in the past, this provision of legitimacy has been visible
through the involvement of officers and politicians in the appointment
and promotion of staff, particularly senior staff. But legitimacy is also
bestowed, as it were, along with training and professional development
monies and with special projects and initiatives.

Our lengthy introduction is at last complete. What is an LEA? — An LEA
is a complex organisation which (a) receives and processes information;
(b) receives and distributes money; and (c) receives and bestows legitimacy. What is an LEA policy statement? — It is a statement of the
mental framework according to which information will be processed,
and of the basic values and principles according to which money and
legitimacy will be distributed and their use monitored. What, then, are
the potential uses of a policy statement on anti-racist and multicultural
education? — Seven main points are here considered.

But first, we need to emphasise that an LEA policy is not only nor
primarily a set of instructions to schools. It may well have the gram-
matical form of such a directive and it may well be understood (and,
probably, resented) as a directive. But essentially, to repeat, it is a
statement about how the LEA itself intends to act and to think, not —
despite appearances — a statement about how others are expected to act
and think. Whether or not it is 'implemented' (though the customary
distinction between 'formulation' and 'implementation' is itself false in
many ways, as the following paragraphs here show) is first and foremost
a question about what happens within the LEA as a complex organisation, and within the support services over which it has direct control,
not about what happens in schools.

The first potential use of a policy statement, and in the light of of the
preceding discussion most obviously, is that it may lead directly to the
provision of new real resources or the re-direction of existing ones.
Either way, second, it may establish how the authority will monitor and
evaluate the use which schools and colleges make of the resources which

171

are granted to them, and it may therefore indicate to schools and colleges what they need or may need to do in order to guarantee for themselves a continuing supply of the maximum possible amount of resources from the authority. Third, by establishing the key terms and concepts of rational debate, it may affect the climate of opinion in the authority — the informal organisational culture and also the formal agendas and priorities of committees and working parties.

Fourth, it may be a useful resource for individual teachers and groups of teachers who are working and arguing for change in their own institutions —it does this by providing legitimacy for them and so helping them to have a rational and serious hearing from their colleagues. Fifth, it may be an indication to teachers of the perspectives and expertise they will need to develop if they are to gain promotion to senior posts. Sixth, it may be a resource for pressure groups and campaigns, for it may help them to structure their demands in such a way that the authority has no choice but to listen to them. In this latter respect an LEA policy statement is a kind of petard by which an LEA consciously and publicly seeks to be hoisted; a deliberate, calculated hostage to fortune; a stick with which it invites people to beat its own back. Seventh, it may lead to structural and organisational change in the LEA's committee structure or in the structuring of the bureaucracy.

These are potential uses, it must be emphasised, not actual ones: the recurring word throughout the previous paragraphs was 'may', not 'is'. If the potential values are to be realised in practice, there are important points to consider about how a policy statement is prepared, formulated and publicised. Five are considered here.

First, there is a need for a lengthy and broad-based process of consultation and — more accurately — negotiation. There are certain LEAs, so it is rumoured, where the policy statement on multicultural education was jotted on the back of an envelope one evening whilst the author was watching *Blankety Blank* on television, slipped then by a colleague into the appendix of a report to the Education Committee on a wholly unrelated subject, and sent out to schools in the last week of July. Alternatively and preferably there needs to be the exhausting — and, yes, stressful, painful and tearful — process of real consultation, real negotiation: drafting committees, discussion papers, public meetings, press releases and coverage, one-day conferences, specialist seminars, serious research, deputations, petitions, minuted resolutions, formal submissions; and argument, argument, argument, much of it impassioned and angry, in countless staffrooms and committee rooms, and in homes and pubs, and on the street.

If indeed a statement is drawn up through a process of consultation and negotiation, it should be seen and read as such by academic observers and researchers. It is like the frozen frame of a film : not comprehensible unless it is contextualised in what has gone before. Negotiation involves an untidy ebb and flow of compromises and concessions, artfulness and persuasiveness, private agendas and economies with the truth. All too often academic observers and researchers study and criticise the text of LEA policy statements, and sometimes indeed ridicule them, as if they were private essays written by undergraduates rather than the products of bargaining and negotiation that they are, formulated collectively by people with a variety of ideological positions and short-term priorities, each trying to get the best possible deal and settlement from their own point of view.[4]

Second, the statement must be owned by the people who are going to use it as a resource in their own arguing, advocacies and campaigning. It is crucial that they should feel that it is their own, something they have won, not something handed down as a sop or fiat, or as a piece of condescending largesse, from above. Third, the statement must retain a high profile after it has been formulated and promulgated. For example, it should frequently feature as a reference point in inservice training and should be issued as a matter of course to all new members of staff, including in particular, but not only, all new headteachers, and to all new school governors.

Fourth, it is of course essential that the actual content and terminology should be considered very closely. In Berkshire we chose to place political concepts rather than cultural concepts at centre-stage: concepts of equality, freedom and justice, and therefore also concepts of discrimination and prejudice.[5] It was only within this wider political framework that we referred to essential matters to do with ethnicity, with language, with personal and collective cultural identity, with religious faith and tradition, and so on. Further, we attempted to define all the key terms of the debate, not just use them as rhetorical shorthand. At the same time we aimed to avoid connotations and usages associated with any one section of the party-political spectrum. To what extent we succeeded in all this, and whether we were right to try in such endeavours in the first place, are questions which will be decided by history.

Fifth and finally, an apparently trivial point which may in fact be very important: the wretched thing should be at least conventionally, and at best elegantly, constructed and written. Distinctions should be logical, as should juxtapositions and conjoinings; spelling should be correct (the task is combating racism, not combatting) and so should usage (phenomena is plural); repetitions should be avoided; subordinate clauses should be scanty; the passive voice should not be used if the active is available; verbs are preferable to abstract nouns; words derived from Anglo-Saxon are always preferable, if they exist, to words derived from Latin and French; semi-colons have their uses. Every word in the statement should be necessary. And every sentence in the statement should be sayable; it should have the sound and the sinews of speech.

Yes, this is all by way of saying that you need a goddam belle-lettrist or belle-lettriste on your drafting committee; plus also someone capable of holding down a job on, let us say, *The Daily Mirror*; plus someone who had the misfortune in their youth to go to a grammar school or, at least, to study linguistic philosophy at an oldish university; plus several sceptical and nit-picking bloody amateurs, totally unafraid to ask what self-styled specialists may consider to be silly questions, over and over and over again. You are involved in what T S Eliot called the intolerable wrestle with words and meanings — though in a committee room and debating chamber rather in some lonely garret somewhere — and like a poet your drafting sub-committee is:

> *Trying to learn to use words, and every attempt*
> *Is a wholly new start, and a different kind of failure*
> *Because one has only learnt to get the better of words*
> *For the thing one no longer has to say, or the way in which*
> *One is no longer disposed to say it.*[6]

Words don't change the world, no. Actions and banknotes speak louder. But words do have their part to play. There are important reasons why we should devote time and energy to ensuring that the words we choose and use are as satisfactory as possible. First, a small point but not trivial: some of our conservative and New Right critics see themselves as defenders and guardians of, amongst other things, literary culture: we score needless own goals in our dealings with them if we use slipshod phrasings and ill-digested jargonese. Second, literary culture is indeed worth defending and nourishing, and we should not allow it to be appropriated by the Right. The language of Shakespeare and Jane Austen, of Blake and Orwell, is an essential and precious heritage for us to draw on in the building of a just and equal multi-racial society in Britain in the 1990s and beyond. We betray this heritage insofar as we couch our policy statements on race equality in newspeak, doublethink and gobblydegook.

For, third, clear thinking and careful writing are of moral and political significance. The task of dismantling racism is indeed, amongst other things, a linguistic task: it involves creating, learning, rehearsing and using a new language. New forms of currency and fluency. Insofar as the message we communicate is business as usual — and that is precisley the message communicated by muddled language! — we do not build confidence and commitment, and ensure on the contrary that no change really takes place.

Perfect verbal clarity, however, is an ideal to strive for, not a goal ever to attain. In the last line of the section in *Four Quartets* from which I quoted, Eliot has two key and careful puns. They are respectively on the words 'trying' and 'rest'. Each of these expresses, in context, both humility and determination, both docility and daring. The word 'trying' has 'achieving' as one of its alternatives, and in this respect its choice implies humility and docility. But also it is an alternative to 'comfortable', and there is determination and daring in the poet's embracing of unease, dis-ease, an unending deal of toil and trouble. 'Rest' can mean 'remainder', and there is humility and docility in the poet's turning away from everything which is not connected to the business of writing poetry — his turning from things like politics, money, revolution, real change. But 'rest' may also mean 'repose', and there is determination and daring in his turning from peace, from sleep, from an easy life. As drafters of policy statements on race equality, and also in the even more important work of actually building and maintaining race equality, we could do worse, much worse, than be inspired by poets:

For us there is only the trying. The rest is not our business.

16. Believing Enough?
— fragments for a memoir

The distinctive feature of the Berkshire race policy was that it put concepts of equality and justice at centre-stage, and tried to explicate them. It was drawn up, together with its supporting documentation, through a lengthy — and at times enormously untidy, heart-rending, infuriating, hilarious, enervating, energising — consultative process. To be actively present at the centre of such a process was an incredible privilege, because of the comrades, friends and colleagues with whom one was in daily contact. Also it was to be frequently cast into anger, despair and dereliction, and this too, frankly, was less to do with one's opponents and critics than with the comrades, friends and colleagues with whom one was in daily contact. Some of your closest allies were other people's most unlovely enemies; some of the people you yourself most admired and respected apparently had feelings only of resentment, criticism and hostility towards you; even when you were at your weakest and most broken, people assumed that you had some sort of amazing Grand Plan in your mind's eye, full of strategies, gambits, ploys and manoeuvres, and lit by brightly coloured goals on the horizon which you alone could see somewhere ahead.

A close colleague gave me at one stage a copy of Horses Make a Landscape Look More Beautiful *by Alice Walker. Her simple inscription in it — 'To Robin, for believing enough' — moved me to compile this sequence of notes and memories, to share amongst a small number of my closest friends and colleagues. Behind the scenes, behind the public persona, I was wanting to say, these were some of the things which were happening, these were some of the doubts and difficulties, some of the anxieties and self-pity, this was some of the pain. Also, this was some of the solace and reassurance, these were some of the sources of hope and persistence, this was some of what the believing entailed.*

The fragments are arranged in chronological order, from September 1979 through to October 1985.

* * * * *

1   A memoir, says the dictionary, is 'a record of events, history written from personal knowledge or special sources of information.'

2   His first day in the new job, the first Monday in September, 1979. A morning of files, documents and papers, and a whirl of introductions, smiles and handshakes. At lunchtime a traditional collective gathering of colleagues in the local pub, to mourn the end of the summer and to mark the start of the new school year. Grey suits, suntans, gin and tonics, pork pies. Masses of further introductions. 'Welcome,' said someone. 'No, don't tell me who you are. I know. They told me' and he gestured over his shoulder at a group of the grey suits, casually drinking and laughing behind him. 'You're our new man for ...'. He used an extraordinary, an outrageous, an unrepeatable, racist phrase.

3   Those first few weeks, autumn 1979. The headteacher who said casually that West Indian pupils look like gorillas — but don't misunderstand me, Mr. Richardson, I'm very fond of gorillas. I always used to give the gorilla a banana when I went to the zoo.' The headteacher who said: 'I hate immigrants just as much as everybody else, they're ruining my school. But I'm a Christian, and I believe God has chosen Britain — he's going to create in Britain a society in which all races are equal. Not, I very much hope, that he'll let it happen in *my* lifetime'. The headteacher who said his purpose when educating Asian and Afro-Caribbean pupils was entirely clear — 'get rid of their strange and funny ways — their gibberish language, their silly clothes, their awful food, their strange and funny religion.'

4   That recurring phrase used by white teachers everywhere: 'our own children.' Meaning white children.

5   But some of the people he met were marvellous. Very determined, very warm, very resilient, very committed, very brave. It was worth staying.

6   Meeting up with an old friend, recalled in a talk a few days later to the Reading Association for Multiracial Education, November 1979. Her: 'I suppose I ought to congratulate you on your, new, er, now that you're one of the buggers.' Him: 'How do you mean?' Her: 'You're on the other bloody side now, aren't you.' Him: 'Am I?' Her: 'Course you are, now that you're an inspector.' Him: 'I'm an adviser,

not an inspector.' Her: 'Oh Christ don't be so bloody wet, your job is to inspect, regulate, control, patch up the system, keep the show on the road, you're a bureaucrat.' Him: 'Well, I...'

7   Someone in Reading he very much respected, and whose respect he very much wanted. 'We're very disappointed, Robin. A lot of people worked very hard, for a very long time, to get your post created, and we're very disappointed. You're a very dangerous person.'

8   In an article about Berkshire written in 1980 the authors said : 'The role of the Education Department's multi-racial adviser appears to be to control the channels of communication, and to divert discussion onto a narrow view of multicultural education and attitude and curriculum change, rather than the promotion of structural changes within the education system.'[8]

9   They also said that the County Council is dominated by a small group, an oligarchy, of councillors, and referred to 'the long-standing weakness and deference of the officers.' The conclusion of their article was that 'Education is a contest, with its participants selected onto different tracks carrying different weights, jumping different hurdles, and with different destinations. Educational policies and institutional practices create not only class inequalities, but also inequalities between black, brown and white people.'

10 In 1980-81 teaching a fifth-year class one afternoon a week at a secondary school. The day Samantha strolled across the classroom to the wastepaper basket, and then with studied swaying of her hips back to her desk. 'I've got a sexy walk, haven't I?' — 'Yes' — 'I've got big tits, haven't I?' — 'Samantha, you're trying to embarrass me. But you can't, you know, you can't embarrass me.' — 'Want to bet?' Sudden silence in the classroom, everyone alert. 'Yes, I don't mind betting. The fact is, Samantha, you can't embarrass me.' Massively complete silence in the classroom. Then very calmly, very deliberately, very ruthlessly, she proceeded to embarrass him.

11 Summer 1981, a meeting of community representatives in the Director's office. 'We don't *want* multicultural education', said someone, pounding the table. 'We want equality.'

12 Samantha had been excluded from all lessons because she had said something very, very rude, he was told, to the R.E. teacher, something so rude that the R.E. teacher couldn't repeat it. Samantha spent

many hours writing in a school exercise book and brought it to him. Shyly but also defiantly. Poignant, and poignantly derivative. 'Love is not just happiness, it's hurting, pain and loneliness... I'm sorry I loved you/I'm sorry I cared/I'm sorry for thinking/My illusions were shared... They call us niggers/Don't they know/it was them who brought us here/many years ago... I wish I was high in the sky/So I could not hear the word "Good-bye"/Cause I know we have to part/And I will die of a broken heart.'

13   Samantha took her 16+ exams in summer 1981, and so did his own daughter, Rachel. For them, and for an audience of their age- group at a school prize-giving and speech-day, he wrote: 'This generation was at the height of its powers from about the year 2010 onwards. Like their parents thirty years earlier, when they for their part had been at the height of their powers, they worked on the issues of their world — issues of conflict and power. And they worked on issues in their families and private lives — issues to do similarly with conflict and power, and with the closing of prison-house shades, the closing of the gates of heaven, the closing of history's accounts. This generation was all dead by about the year 2040. It didn't solve all the problems of the world, nor all the problems it encountered in its marriages and family life. No generation ever does. But it worked on those problems. That is why today we must praise, why today we must thank, why today we must bless, this generation.'

14   *Education for Equality: a paper for discussion in Berkshire*, was published in summer 1982. The press conference to launch it, the Windsor Room, Shire Hall. Bored cub reporters from the *Maidenhead Advertiser*, the *Newbury Gazette*, the *Wokingham Times*, the *Slough Observer*, the *Reading Chronicle*, etc, sat around. The guest speaker was for some reason (hay fever?) wearing sunglasses in that darkish solemn room with the sombre photographs of various civic digni- taries on its panelled walls. 'We must contextualise this document,' he said, holding it up. 'We must contextualise this document in the longstanding and worldwide bitter struggle of black people against racism, capitalism and imperialism'. The cub reporters, blankly dropping their pencils.

15   Important to reorganise the language centres — to get their talents, expertise, commitment, perspective, energy, out into the schools. But painful — the changing of boundaries, the uprooting, the ambi- guities, the fluidity. A teacher who seemed even more anxious than

most saying she would need a very, very detailed contract. Suppose it was snowing one morning, and she couldn't get to school on time. 'Don't worry, don't worry; said the education officer handling all the administration. 'Everything will be all right. And of course we'll have a clause in your contract about the snow.' He looked at her gravely and with huge reassurance. 'And we'll give it a special name for you. We'll call it the Santa Clause.'

16   One of Berkshire's most energetic, most determined, most skilled, most affirmative, most resilient teachers. The morning a straw, in the form of a terse memo from Shire Hall, broke briefly even that brave camel's back.

17   Wendy Robinson writes : 'Many things only take shape for us in an atmosphere of trust provided by someone who really can and will listen. We can listen to what is said — to what is actually given, open and apparent between us in the situation — and respond with all that we are and can appropriately give at that moment so that the other is left free and yet is confirmed in their existence and potentiality. We can try to listen to what is *not* being said — what is being left out, hidden, kept back, not yet formulated — perhaps because there is not yet enough trust in our presence in the situation to allow certain things to be said. We must respond to that too. With all the tacit sensitivity we have, in an enabling way, towards the future, respecting to the uttermost the secrets and privacy of the other.'[2]

18   From the Berkshire policy statement : 'The relationship between equality and justice is circular. Justice is the means by which equality is both achieved and maintained. Equality is not only the consequence of justice but also its basis and surest guarantee.'

19   An education officer: 'They had riots in Brixton, they had riots in Bristol, they had riots in Liverpool, they had riots in Manchester, they had riots all over the bloody place. But we didn't have riots in Berkshire. For me that says something.'

20   Paulo Freire writes : 'While some revolutionary leaders consider dialogue with the people a bourgeois and reactionary activity, the bourgeoisie regard dialogue between the oppressed and the revolutionary leaders as a very real danger to be avoided. One of the methods of manipulation is to inoculate individuals with the bourgeois appetite for personal success. This manipulation is sometimes

carried out directly by the elites and sometimes indirectly, through populist leaders... The populist leader who rises from this process is an ambiguous being, an amphibian who lives in two elements... Since the populist leader simply manipulates, instead of fighting for authentic popular organisation, this type of leader serves the revolution little if at all.'[3] Cf, perhaps, some of our community leaders.

21 A very dear friend writes with a birthday greeting, November 1983: 'There is a problem with teaching, schools, educational institutions, families, governments, and notions of political education. The problem is patriarchy. All men benefit economically and politically from this system so it follows that however gentle and reasonable they may be as individuals, men themselves are a problem. There is a fox in every hen house. Men continue to define and interpret the world for most women and enjoy the lion's share of physical, emotional, psychological and intellectual servicing. Paradoxically they are squandering the very resources that were so painfully and creatively developed to resist them. The kissing has to stop.'

22 Letter to a university-based researcher, January 1984, about an article the latter had written in the *Times Education Supplement* 'To ask "is it realistic to expect policy statements to effect changes in classroom practice?" is like asking, when one goes to the theatre, "is it realistic to expect an actor whispering on the stage to be heard at the back of the gallery?" *Of course* it isn't realistic. The theatre audience is familiar, however, with the convention of the stage whisper. The actor is pretending to whisper to other people on the stage but is in reality — and this convention is entirely understood and accepted —speaking to the gallery. With LEA policy statements the convention is precisely the other way round. The LEA is pretending to speak to people a long way away ("Berkshire County Council requires all its education institutions and services to...") but is in reality speaking to itself. Or rather, it is speaking *intra muros*, within its own four walls... The purpose of the internal LEA debate is to release and re-direct resources, including legitimacy, and to effect change in the LEA organisation itself.'

23 The strenuous striving amongst certain community leaders to retain or retrieve pre-migration status. Cf, perhaps, the opening page of *Midnight's Children*: 'Time (having no further use for me) is running out... I have no hope of saving my life, nor can I count on having even a thousand nights and a night. I must work fast, faster than

Scheherazade, if I am to end up meaning — yes, meaning — something. I admit it : above all things, I fear absurdity.'[4]

24 Chris Mullard writes : 'The real agents of the delegitimisation of black resistance and legitimisation of racism... are located in the very creation itself of a black professional class of race workers, and the way in which this class has been expanded, mobilised, positioned and used by the state.'[5] Cf our new appointments?

25 He wore a lapel badge at the Notting Hill Carnival, 1984 — Black People Support The Miners.

26 From a memorandum written to himself, 1984. 'The essential educational task is to equip the oppressed with words — the ABC, the first two Rs, Shakespeare and all that. Part of the essential political task is to provide them with platforms — a hearing in the places and spaces where a rule is to listen. Words + platforms = communicative competence. Often you yourself should be silent, or at least your memoranda should be unmemorable. But sometimes you may speak, you may use both words and platforms Choose them, choose them with care.'

27 Looking up from the communion rail one Sunday to the commanding resurrection appearance above. 'My name is Allah, too. Go and knock on the door tomorrow of Mr Mohammed Afzal, Slough Islamic Trust.' How absolutely and utterly daft and ridiculous, in so many ways. But he went.

28 'How's life?' This was spring 1985. 'It's er, it's interesting.' 'Yes, it's interesting, isn't it, being killed.'

29 Weeping through the film because knowing how the book ended, and thinking of various failed or failing friendships. 'The horses didn't want it — they swerved apart; the earth didn't want it, sending up rocks through which the riders must pass single file; the temples, the tank, the jail, the palace, the birds, the carrion, the Guest House... : they didn't want it, they said in their hundred voices, "No, not there."'[6]

30 From *Small World* by David Lodge, read in 1985. ' "Habit ruins everything in the end, doesn't it? Perhaps that's what we're all looking for — desire undiluted by habit." — "The Russian Formalists had a word for it," said Morris. — "I'm sure they did," said

Philip. "But it's no use telling me what it was, because I'm sure to forget it." — "Ostranemie," said Morris. "Defamiliarisation. It was what they thought literature was all about. 'Habit devours objects, clothes, furniture, one's wife, and the fear of war ... Art exists to help us recover the sensation of life.' Viktor Shklovsky." '[7]

31 The *Daily Telegraph* in summer 1985, referring selectively to an article he had written in summer 1982. ' "Your commitment should be to justice, not to truth," Berkshire schoolteachers were instructed by an adviser to the county educational authority. The teachers are told they must be on the side of the worker against employer, black against white, female against male; that conflict is the supreme goal. This is not what citizens of Berkshire pay rates and elect councillors for.'

32 From something he wrote, entitled *Anti-Racist Education — a memorandum to white friends* : 'Personal confessions and references are occasionally necessary but always dicey. Necessary, because we are otherwise in danger of being destructively intolerant, ungracious, abrasive, ill-tempered. Dicey, because they plunge us into the danger of being priggish, pharisaical and self-indulgent, and of losing all sense of seriousness, toughness and urgency. Further, there is the danger of forgetting that the essential task is structural change, not personal.'

33 One of his last evenings, October 1985, a social occasion. 'We're glad you're going, at long last. We only hope you don't do as much damage to the communities in Brent as you've done here in Berkshire. They're not as tolerant in Brent as we are, you know. They'll burn the whole place down if you do to them what you've done to us.'

34 A Hasidic tale. The Rabbi Zusya said, 'At the end I shall be asked not "Why were you not Moses?" but "Why were you not Zusya?"'[8]

35 Thomas Merton writes : 'Whether the plane pass by tonight or tomorrow, whether there be cars on the winding road or no cars, whether people speak in the field, whether there be a radio in the house or not, the tree brings forth her blossoms in silence. Whether the house be empty or full of children, whether the people go off to town or work with tractors in the fields, whether the liner enters the

harbour full of tourists or full of soldiers, the almond tree brings forth her fruit in silence.'[9]

36 The gift was inscribed so simply. 'For believing enough.'

37 Alice Walker writes : 'I think of Rebecca. "Mama, are you a racist?" she asks. And I realise I have badmouthed white people once too often in her presence. Years ago I would have wondered how white people have managed to live all these years with this question from their children; or, how did they train their children not to ask. Now I think how anti-racism like civil rights or affirmative action helps white people too... Talking to Rebecca about race almost always guarantees a headache. But that is a small price for the insight and clarity she brings.'[10]

38 Alice Walker adds : 'Surely the earth can be saved for Rebecca.'

MEMORANDA ON POINTS ARISING

Memoranda on points arising

This book draws towards a close with a series of brief memoranda jotted at various stages during the 1980s. They were in the first instance written for a variety of different audiences, and are therefore in a range of different voices and styles, and have a range of different emphases. But all, in their various ways, re-state the recurring theme of this book as a whole — that we need to be seeking a dynamic synthesis between learner-centred education and education for equality. The search for such a synthesis is a challenge, as these memoranda between them show, to both of the fields concerned. Each needs to listen to and to learn from the other, and to dare to change in the light of what is heard and taken on board.

The first piece, From the Inner City, *was written for an audience in, as the phrase often is, the white highlands. I had been asked to leave London for a day, and to reflect with a group of educators in a shire authority about the possible implications for themselves of our experience in a place such as Brent.*

The second, What shall we tell the children?, *considers the messages about 'race' and culture which the educational system should be trying to present to pupils and students, both in the formal curriculum and in the hidden curriculum.*

The third, On Anti-racism, *and the fourth,* On Municipal Socialism, *are internal memos written for discussion within four walls. In a sense, it is breaking confidence to publish them at all widely — they* were for private discussion, and to reprint them here may seem like washing dirty linen in public. However, one of their essential themes is that there is a need for greater openness and greater self-criticism, and it is with this theme and concern in mind that they are included here.

The piece entitled Lecturing was originally written for a conference in Australia, and was used to introduce the lecture reprinted elsewhere in this book on The Age of Aquarius. It is a kind of meditation on the delicate and mysterious relationship which obtains between a lecturer and her audience, and may be relevant also - incidentally - to the relationship between author and reader.

Finally, Memorandum to Oppressors. This was originally written as an epilogue for the lecture entitled Learning towards Justice, in Part One. It offers a private code of conduct for anyone who in a racist society is white; in a sexist society is male; in a class society is middle-class; in a hierarchy is rather senior. Its alternative title was, and remains, 'memorandum to myself'.

* * * * *

17. Messages from the inner city

1   The arrival of black pupils and students in British schools and colleges over the last 20 years or so has pressured or required us to make changes, or at least to begin making changes, which educational institutions arguably ought to be making anyway. They include:

- Self-critical focus on educational practices, procedures, assumptions, day-to-day culture, etc, rather than on the supposed deficiencies of learners.

- An emphasis, within the context of assuming that all learners have a right to the same basic and broad core curriculum, on mixed-attainment groupings and classes, and therefore on the practical skills and strategies which teachers need to use and develop in such settings.

- A concern to facilitate access to the same basic core curriculum, and to educational opportunities and institutions, by communicating respect and affirmation for all learners, and to remove or minimise messages which imply a lack of such interest and repect.

- An acknowledgement that for many learners, and for the families and communities to which they belong, a central aspect of their experience, and therefore of the culture they are daily building and renewing, is experience of prejudice and structural discrimination, both overt and covert.

- A focus on selection, advertising and interviewing procedures, and on training and career development patterns and opportunities, to ensure that these do not have the effect of bringing forward only a narrow group of staff (viz mainly white, mainly male) for promotion to senior posts.

- An international or global dimension in much or most of the curriculum — including science, technology and mathematics as well as arts, humanities and literature.

- Less emphasis on dualistic, either-or thinking, and more emphasis on holistic and dialectical thinking, in particular with regard to traditional Western distinctions between fact and value, material and organic, physical and social, mind and body, reason and imagination, masculine and feminine, work and leisure.

- A focus on language studies and language awareness and, within this context, on appropriacy, accent and dialect, and the concepts of 'standard' and 'non-standard'.

- An explicit focus on teaching about concepts such as prejudice, discrimination, racism, racial justice, race equality, etc, within the framework of — amongst other frameworks — social and political education.

2   Educational institutions in mainly white areas need to be very consciously aware, and this awareness needs to be institutionalised into certain formal procedures and formal job descriptions of staff, that their ethnic minority students are likely to be experiencing major pressures as a consequence of white racism.

3   If the messages mentioned above are heeded, large numbers of people are likely to benefit. White people as well as black are damaged by racism. Moreover, it is not possible (or rather, it is not easy, and it is not desirable or likely to be successful) to tackle racism without also tackling other kinds of inequality and disadvantage.

18. What shall we tell the children?

In particular, what shall we say about 'race' and culture?

Quite literally, what are the messages we wish our learners to hear from our lips in formal teaching and informal chats and conversations, and off-the-cuff remarks?

And what do we want them to hear from our silences? And from textbooks, worksheets, overhead transparencies, materials resources of all kinds? And from people we arrange for them to meet from the wider world? And, not least, from each other?

Here, as a first draft for discussion and improvement, is a list of points and messages which seem important with regard to race and racism, and to cultural diversity.

* * * * *

A. 'Race' and Race Relations

1. *'Race'*

   It is not stated or implied that human beings can be divided into biological 'races', and words reflecting this false belief ('Caucasian', 'Asiatic', 'Negro', 'Coloured' etc) are not used.

2. *Opposition to racialism*

   Racialism — the twin false beliefs that (a) races exist and (b) whites are superior — is opposed and criticized, both as personal belief and as political doctrine.

3. *Opposition to racism*

   Racism — the combination of (a) unequal power structures, (b) discriminatory procedures and (c) prejudices — is opposed and criticized.

4. *Migration*

   It is emphasized that black people came to Britain in the 1950s and the 1960s primarily because their labour was needed by the economy. Many were explicitly invited or recruited.

B. References to Black People

(The term 'black' is a political term, not a biological term. Its use implies that racism is the basic phenomenon to be named, not cultural differences, and that opposition to racism is a basic political struggle. In contemporary Britain it refers both to Asian people and to Afro-Caribbean.)

5. *Control and decision-making*

   Black people are shown as in control of their lives and environments, and with intentions, desires and ideals, not merely as passive victims.

6. *Their own words*

   The views and perspectives of black people are presented or quoted in their own terms — literally, in their own words, and in their own categories and definitions.

7. *Everyday life and values*

   There are examples of warmth, care, love, laughter, kindness, in the descriptions of family life and everyday relationships of black people.

C. Aspects of Cultural Diversity

8. *Multicultural, multiracial 'West'*
    Britain and the United States, and also most West European coun-
    tries, are shown as multicultural, multiracial, multilingual, multi-
    faith societies. They are not all-white, not all-Christian, not all
    monolingual.

9. *Meanings*
    Customs, lifestyles, traditions and beliefs in other cultures are
    shown as having value and meaning for the people concerned, not
    as exotic, peculiar or bizarre.

10. *Generalizations*
    Generalizations about all or most people in another country or
    culture are not made or implied. On the contrary there is emphasis
    on diversity within other groups.

11. *One World*
    It is clear that many apparently localized, smallish-scale events in
    the modern world are in fact influenced by, and may themselves
    influence, events and trends elsewhere.

12. *Religion*
    Christianity is not shown as the only true religion, the only source
    of valid religious insight and experience. Religions other than Chris-
    tianity are described in their own terms and categories, not with
    Christian or Western terms.

13. *Interaction and learning*
    People in other countries and cultures are portrayed as people from
    whom 'we' can learn —their values, their experiences of life, their
    insights, their politics.

D. References to the Third World

14. *Poverty and politics*
    It is not implied that poverty is merely the absence of Western goods,
    nor that poverty is mainly a consequence of climate and environ-
    ment, or of ignorance.

15. *Science and technology*
    Scientific and technological achievements are not shown as exclu-
    sively Western or European, either in the past or in the present.

16. *History*

Third World countries and cultures are shown as having a long history and tradition — they were not merely 'discovered' by Europeans.

17. *Liberation and struggle*

Struggles by black and Third World people against oppression are shown and evaluated from their own points of view, not merely dismissed as disorders, riots, revolts, insurrections, etc.

18. *Language*

The language avoids insulting or patronizing terms — for example, 'coloured', 'tribe', 'native', 'primitive', 'hut', 'superstitious', 'witchdoctor', 'chief', 'jabber'.

19. *Heroes and heroines*

People who are considered and admired in Third World countries as heroes and heroines are described in these terms, and their influence and inspiration are clear.

E. References to Particular Issues

20. *Islam*

Islam is shown as a religious tradition of great depth and insight, and as a major cultural influence and civilisation. It is not implied that Muslims are typically 'fundamentalists' or 'fanatics', and terms such as 'the rise of Islam', implying threat, are not used.

21. *South Africa*

It is not implied that apartheid is merely a matter of segregation — separation in housing, cinemas, parks, railways etc. The inequalities and injustices of a political and economic nature are emphasized, and there is reference to South Africa's economic links with Western countries.

F. General References

(These last points are not *directly* related to racism and non-racism. It is probable, however, that a non-racist curriculum will have these features also, at least.)

22. *The role of women*

In all countries and cultures, and at all times in history, women are shown as half of the human race, and their work and actions as essential. The word 'man' is not used to refer to all human beings.

197

Traditional gender roles are shown as man-made (sic), not immutable.

23. *Conflict and its resolution*
Human beings frequently, even typically, disagree and dispute with each other, they are in constant conflict. This reality is not glossed over, but resolutions of conflict which are (a) non-violent and (b) just are emphasized also.

24. *The media*
There are frequent reminders that newspapers and television oversimplify and distort — for example by ignoring long-term underlying causes of events, by concentrating on personalities and trivialities, by seeking to entertain rather than to explain, and by flattering and reinforcing the prejudices of the audience.

25. *'Ordinary' people*
The vast majority of human beings are 'ordinary' and always have been — not monarchs, rulers, politicians, aristocracy etc. Their experience and outlook are attended to and respected, both in the past and in the present.

26. *Bias*
Everything is biased. Every book, talk, lesson, course, syllabus and topic in schools is biased, and so is every list such as this.

19. On Anti-racism,
a memorandum amongst friends, 1984

1 Management and de-management

The overall task has been summarised as 'the de-management of racism'. It involves rigorous awareness of how racism operates in each separate institution, but also very considerable management skills and insight. We need to understand deeply the dynamics of organisations, bureaucracies and power-structures, and therefore to sit at the feet of certain people whom some of us naively, and perhaps enviously, despise, viz management specialists and consultants in industry.

2 Structural seedbeds and potential racism

We often make a useful distinction between racism and racialism, and we know that racialism (eg support for fascist organisations) flourishes in certain particular contexts — unemployment, rootlessness, failure, loss of pride and previous identity, and so on. We need a broadly similar theory with regard to racism. Arguably, racism is potential particularly where there are hierarchies, bureaucratic procedures and role-structures, closed systems of organisation, and tightly controlled social boundaries.

3 Personal change theory

We are, we say, concerned basically with structural not personal change. Fair enough. Nevertheless we surely have much to learn from humanistic psychology, and the research done over many years on the circumstances in which people change, if they do, their beliefs and attitudes.

4 Velvet gloves

Anti-racist action in practice may be nothing more sometimes than the rendering of injustice as palatable, gentle, acceptable. There is a frequent tendency to make the acceptable face of injustice a black face: that is, to build a black bourgeoisie to contain and control black youth, and to hold out images of success within the present unjust system. Another force behind the building of a black bourgeoisie is the tendency to buy off or mute certain activist individuals and sectional interests through the distribution of jobs, promotions, grants and patronage.

5 Party politics

Many anti-racists have their heart in, so to speak, the Left place. Here are some provocative propositions about this, for debate:

(i)   Socialism may be necessary, but certainly it is not sufficient, if racism is to be ended.

(ii)   There is a lot of racism in the Labour Party and other parties of the Left.

(iii)   There are many worthwhile things which can and should be done against racism without waiting for a socialist transformation of society as a whole — which does not appear very imminent.

(iv)   White anti-racists are betraying black people insofar as they permit themselves to be labelled as loony left, trendies, rent-a-crowd, etc.

(v)   All-party and cross-party alliances and coalitions on 'race' are by and large to be cautiously welcomed rather than squeamishly avoided.

(vi)   Our political opponents will be given an unnecessary advantage against us if we do not openly acknowledge that 'race' issues are politically controversial.

(vii)   Can we please discuss points such as these amongst ourselves rather more often than we do?

(viii) And discuss too why we so often find such discussion very awkward, even painful, and usually avoid it?

20. Municipal Socialism
— a memorandum *intra muros*, New Year's Day 1989

Space

A week's a long time, yes, in the art of the possible, the heat of the kitchen. Long enough, surely, even amongst all the shaky agreements and unwelcome alliances, the craft of fixing, dealing, trimming and choosing, the calculating economies with truth and, even though it's no longer leap year, to find space for some real debate, real deliberation, patient sifting and exploration of alternative perceptions, alternative paths?

Polish

Decent P.R. is a simple routine duty, not a corrupt or corrupting luxury. And certainly it should never be an afterthought. The right words in the right order, and the right place. The right time, the right person. Poetry and prose, journalism and philosophy, artfulness and artistry. Package, polish, massage, gloss: it is, if you love yourself as your neighbour, a simple moral duty.

Learning

Mistakes happen. Also — which is not the same thing, true, but just as important — they are perceived to happen. Perceived by our opponents, of course, but also, after all, by ourselves. We need not be swift to debate with our opponents or to conduct post-mortems in public. But internal debate, rueful yet not recriminatory, is essential. Learning to be wise, or just wiser, after the event — essential need.

Ecology
Green's not red, but it's not blue either — yet. Both pragmatism and principle demand a hearing for ecology, the science of home-making, a science not only of seals and forests but also of power and persons, a political science: a hearing for networks not hierarchies, for the small that is beautiful, for the organisational and political correlatives of quantum physics, holistic medicine, alternative technology, earth-friendly husbandry, new age spirituality, the whole new paradigm.

Reasons
Mockery and disinformation against us are as inevitable as resistance, opposition, silencing, repression. But we begin to deserve the loony label ('affected with the kind of insanity that was supposed to depend on changes of the moon' — *Oxford Dictionary of English Etymology;* 'maniac, nut case, nutter, psychopath' — the *New Collins Thesaurus)* if we cannot or will not argue, reason, remonstrate, defend, unpack, work out, explain. Both to others and to ourselves.

21 Lecturing: What is a lecture?

A lecture is a frozen frame in the film
of one person's living and working,
loving and wrestling,
a film of their blessings and failures,
affirmations and surrenders,
journeys and unfolding.

The frozen frame is composed —
crafted, shaped, moulded, organised.

The purpose is to be a resource —
a resource for other people's films,
other people's journeys,
other people's crafting, shaping, moulding.

A lecture is also a space,
an arena or ground where people meet,
where they examine a frozen frame,
and use it, if they can,
as a resource in their own journeying.

It follows that a lecturer
is like a cinema manager as well as a film director,
a theatre manager as well as an actress,
a publisher as well as an author,
a gallery owner as well as a painter,
a midwife as well as a mother,
a ringmaster as well as a clown.

In this shaping and composing
of the product,
and of the space,
the minimal duties
are courtesy and craft.

With good fortune and unmerited blessing
there may be also,
of a kind,
love and art.

Courtesy, craft/love, art:
the second pair, you know,
are not merely more of,
an expansion of,
the first —

they may sometimes be,
in reality or in appearance,
in opposition.

22 Memorandum to oppressors

Notes on terminology

A relationship, interaction or social system is *oppressive* if it involves gains, benefits and advantages for some at the cost of losses, frustrations and harm for others. *Oppressors* are individuals, groups and classes who have more than their fair share of gains. The *oppressed* are those who have more than their fair share of losses. The archetypal oppressor lives in the northern hemisphere; is middle-class; is white; is male; has a senior position in a hierarchical institution.

Whether you are an oppressor or not depends on your location in an oppressive structure, not on your intention or wish. The question is not whether you wish to be an oppressor but what are you doing to transform the structure.

1 Seek confrontation and opposition

> Over and over again you get things wrong. You are deformed and blinkered by your location and experience. You cannot trust yourself, not your eyesight, nor your judgement. Seek out people who have very different location and experience — that is, the oppressed — and heed their critiques, criticism and challenges.

2 Flattery and chance

> Day in day out people flatter you. For you control goods and goodies which they desire. The consequence of this flattery is that you suppose with pride that you are in your present position through your own merit and achievement. But no, you are where you are through chance, not choice. You live in a society in which

people with certain chance attributes (gender, race, class, nation) get rewarded and flattered.

3 Don't divide and rule

There is a diversity of interests, concerns and priorities amongst the oppressed, and many are prevented — for example by the mass media and by the educational system — from knowing the dimensions and contours of their oppression. You must not take, let alone seek, advantage from this diversity and lack of awareness.

4 Selfishness and self-interest

All human beings pursue and defend their self-interest, yes of course, and all in this do things which are morally wrong. But only oppressors have the power to define which wrong actions are crimes. Also oppressors have the power to define the signs, symbols and conventions of courtesy and considerateness. In consequence of this dual power, oppressors typically think they are morally superior to the oppressed. They are not. Never forget this.

5 Positive action

Regardless of any formal equal opportunities policies which may be around, you should be engaging continually in positive discrimination. Do everything you can to distribute power, influence, resources and goods to or towards the oppressed. You will often have to do this covertly rather than openly: so be it.

6 Acknowledgements

Everyone peppers their discourse and conversation with bibliographical footnotes — references to people from whom they have learnt, and/or people who are big names. Make sure that you yourself, in your footnotes and references, give credit only to the oppressed. This means — amongst other things — that you should indeed reckon to have your mind nurtured only or mainly by the oppressed.

7 The climate of oppressor opinion

Transformation of the system will come, if it comes at all, from the oppressed. You yourself have only a small part to play. But one thing you can do, and should do, is criticise, cajole, badger, pester, speak out, in the forums, informal as well as formal, of the oppressor. But watch out: don't let them dress you in the cap and bells of a court jester or in the stiff righteous collar of a prig.

8 Double-agents

As long as you stay where you are it is possible that you will work, whether you wish to or intend to or not, against the interests of the oppressed. For example, and in particular, you are part of the velvet glove round the oppressor's iron fist; you may be containing resistance, buying time for the oppressor, that's all. One consequence of this is that you have no right or reason to expect gratitude, sympathy or trust from the oppressed.

9 Lifestyle

Look at your possessions, your personal time, your personal space and mobility: you are very comfortable, and very corrupt. You cannot completely change your lifestyle as long as you stay in your location. But you can keep it modest and frugal; you can share it; you can treat it lightly; and you can — and you must — risk it.

10 Words and platforms

The essential educational task is to equip the oppressed with words — the ABC, the first two Rs, Shakespeare and all that. Part of the essential political task is to provide them with platforms — a hearing in the places and spaces where a rule is to listen. (Words + platforms = communicative competence). Often you yourself should be silent, or at least your memoranda should be unmemorable. But sometimes you may speak, you may use both words and platforms. Choose them, choose them with care.

Notes and References

1 Daring to be a Teacher

1   *Petals of Blood*, p. 21.

2   From the stage version created by Jean-Claude Carriere for Peter Brook, p.105.

3   *The Anatomy Lesson*, p.37.

4 Learning towards Justice

1   From Salman Rushdie's book about his visit to Nicaragua, *The Jaguar Smile*, p.40.

2   Quoted by Rushdie, op cit., p.42.

3   *Pedagogy of the Oppressed*, p.43 of the Penguin edition. Freire is himself partly quoting from Erich Fromm's *The Heart of Man*. The quotation from Gandhi is from Raghavan Iyer's book about Gandhi's life and thought, p. 252.

4   Bertolt Brecht, *Collected Poems*.

5   Paulo Freire's best known work is *Pedagogy of the Oppressed*. His book for educators and politicians in Guinea Bissau, *Pedagogy in Process*, describes his ideas in easily accessible form. *Education: the Practice of Freedom*, also published under the title *Education for Critical Consciousness*, is rather technical, but usefully and interestingly includes a set of the pictures which Freire used when 'encoding' or 'posing' problems for his learners to name and to analyse in group discussion. Similarly Cynthia Brown's pamphlet, *Literacy in 30 Hours*, includes a set of the pictures. One of the clearest expositions of Freire's thought readily available is Brian Wren's *Education for Justice*.

6   Three of these terms — conforming, reforming and transforming — are taken from the work of William Smith and his colleagues, who applied Freirean methods and approaches in a series of adult education projects and programmes which they undertook in the early 1970s in Ecuador. In the address to headteachers, *You Haven't Lost Yet, Kids*, the three approaches are referred to simply as perspectives A, B and C respectively.

7   Reprinted from the World Studies Project's handbook for teachers, *Learning for Change*.

209

8   The whole story is a kind of monologue. It devastatingly but with great sympathy and love shows how, in Freirean terminology, the oppressor may be 'housed' within the consciousness of the oppressed. The story is in Katherine Mansfield's collection *The Garden Party*.

9   From *The Fire Next Time* by James Baldwin, p.84 of the Penguin edition.

10   Quoted by Matthew Fox in *Original Blessing*, p.287.

11   Freire says of Che Guevara that 'it was his own humility and capacity to love that made possible his communion with the people'(*Pedagogy of the Oppressed*, p. 138), and 'trusting the people is the indispensable precondition for revolutionary change' (p.36). Brian Wren emphasises the need for 'a profound faith in people - in their potential to know, discover, create, and give something significant to the world and to each other' (*Education for Justice*, p.23). Steve Biko wrote that 'all our action is usually joint community oriented action rather than the individualism which is the hallmark of the capitalist approach. We always refrain from using people as stepping stones. Instead we are prepared to have a much slower progress in an effort to make sure that all of us are marching to the same tune'. (Biko, 1979, p.42.)

12   Reprinted in *Why We Can't Wait*, p.79

13   There are many vivid illustrations of this choice in fiction. For example, most of the protagonists of Iris Murdoch's novels are members of the oppressor class who experience in their own private and personal lives the moral choice between the despair and emptiness of 'deforming' and the love and creativity involved in 'transforming'. In her philosophical commentary *The Sovereignty of Good* Iris Murdoch comments: 'Where strong emotions of sexual love, or of hatred, resentment or jealousy are concerned, "pure will" can usually achieve little. It is small use telling oneself "Stop being in love, stop feeling resentment, be just." What is needed is a reorientation which will provide an energy of a different kind, from a different source.' Such reorientation, or re-direction of attention, is an essential component of 'transformation'.

5 The Age of Aquarius

1   From *The New Confessions* by William Boyd, p.170.

2   The image is suggested by Gary Zukav in his overview of the new physics entitled *The Dancing Wu Li Masters*, p. 114.

3   For example, Matthew Fox and Brian Swimme, in their 'manifesto for a global civilisation': 'The fundamental symbol for the classical scientific world view was the billiard table with the billiard balls glancing off one another. The fundamental symbol for the world view that has emerged from twentieth century physics is that of the musical symphony...For with the symphony we are compelled to begin with the wholeness of the music altogether before we attempt any analysis or discussion... the emerging global civilisation is grounded on the understanding that the world is an undivided whole.' (p.35)

4   Starhawk's celebration of the feminine and of the wisdom of women, *Dreaming the Dark*, is necessarily and simultaneously also, she says, a celebration of interdependence as distinct from hierarchy and 'mastery'. The first principle of women's wisdom, she says, is that 'all things are interconnected, all is relationship'(p.44). Jill Blackmore's critique of male-dominated educational institutions is a critique of, amongst much else, particular forms of scientist epistemology : 'The masculine image of leadership in education is ...maintained by its ideological underpinnings of dominant theories of a value-free science and liberal political theory... Founded upon a positivistic epistemology which separates the body from the mind, which extracts feeling and emotion from the material, leadership is defined to be a rational, cognitive process... The lack of women in higher positions can be excused within such a theoretical

framework as a consequence of women's irrationality, subjectivity and emotionality'. (In Smyth, ed, 1989, p.119).

5   From the poem 'Cypress and Cedar', by Tony Harrison, *Selected Poems*, p.203. The two woods are signs and reminders for Harrison of many other pairings also, including masculine and feminine ('one half we'll call the female, one the male, /though neither essence need, in love, prevail') and immensity and particularity, ancient mythology and mysticism on the one hand and his own very contemporary poem on the other..

6   From the story *Studies in the Park*, in the collection *Games at Twilight*, p. 29.

7   In our choosing of the term 'unlimited potential' in Brent we were influenced in particular by the work and achievements of Reuven Feuerstein. Howard Sharron's book, *Changing Children's Minds*, provides a fine overview.

8   The terms here are of course echoes from the conforming, reforming, deforming, transforming framework proposed in the chapter entitled *Learning towards Justice*. The four stances can be adopted towards small and finite occasions and institutions, for example conferences, as well as towards the social order as a whole.

9   From *All God's Children Need Travelling Shoes*, p.207.

6. Bricks in the Wall

1   The ruling party in Berkshire, guided by the New Right nationallay, attempted in 1987/88, to abrogate the policy on race equality which the Council had formulated and promulgated earlier in the decade. The ensuing campaign to save the policy was successful, and its success was probably due at least in part to the fact that the policy statement itself could not be easily rubbished as intellectually vacuous. The account of 'letterism' in this essay is an expansion of the Berkshire policy paper, particularly of its basic threefold distinction between structures, procedures and attitudes. There is reference in the essay entitled *Worth the Paper it's Written On?* to how the policy was formulated.

2   Dervla Murphy, *Tales from Two Cities*, p.85. Structuralist views of racism are provided by all the essays in *The Empire Strikes Back*, compiled by the Centre for Contemporary Cultural Studies in Birmingham. Particularly relevant to education are Errol Lawrence's paper 'Just plain common sense', and Hazel Carby's 'Schooling in Babylon'. See also Sivanandan's work, for example his seminal 1983 article.

3   This threefold distinction is central to the work of Robert Haynes, in his theoretical model of local government. (Haynes 1980). Also the emphasis here on the overlap of structure and culture recalls the analyses made by observers of international relations — Johan Galtung, for example, distinguishes between 'ideological power' (culture), 'remunerative power', and 'punitive power' (the control of goods and bads which is the basis of structure) (Galtung, 1973).

4   The treatment of race inequality in the media is considered by authors such Cohen and Gardner; John Twitchin (in particular in his 1988 book, which contains many useful suggestions relating to media analysis in schools); and by various authors and groups who have analysed the fabrications of the tabloid press and the New Right with regard to the race equality policies of certain local authorities: Nancy Murray (1989), David Edgar (1987), Jolyon Jenkins (1987), and the Goldsmiths Media Research Group (1987). Chris Searle has analysed and documented in depth *The Sun's* racist reportage and editorial comment. (Murray and Searle, 1989).

5   On 'the shared enterprise of world-making' in everyday conversational life, a seminal paper for sociologists has been 'Marriage and the Construction of Reality' by Peter Berger and Hansfried Kellner. 'The sociology of knowledge', they write, 'must not only be concerned with the great universes of meaning that history offers up for our inspection, but with the many little workshops in which living individuals keep

hammering away at the construction and maintenance of these universes.' (This quotation is on pages 30-31 of *School and Society*, edited by B.R. Cosin et alia). Another 'little workshop' in which human beings 'hammer away' at the construction of shared meanings is of course the school classroom: hence the essential importance of group discussion in school classrooms, as described in greater detail in the essays in this book entitled *How Learners Learn* and *Talking as Equals*. Little workshops are also often dramatised through rituals and ceremonies of various kinds, as for example in office-parties: this point is recalled by the piece in this book entitled *Accustomed As We Are*.

6   John Hodge and his co-authors, in their book on the cultural bases of racism and group expression, quote Frantz Fanon : 'Let us decide not to imitate Europe; let us combine our muscles and our brains in a new direction. Let us try to create the whole man, whom Europe has been incapable of bringing to triumphant birth.' They summarise the argument of their own book as follows: 'The traditional dualism of Western culture is the belief that the universe contains objective and opposing forces of universal good and evil, and that the moral goal of mankind is to enable or insure that the good control the evil...Together, the cultural patterns of traditional Western life make up a dualist culture. Group oppression is an integral part of this traditional attempt to control evil.' (Pages 252-53).

7   There is massive and intricate evidence on all this in *Education for Some*, also known as the Eggleston Report, compiled by John Eggleston with David Dunn and Madhu Anjali. The authors' detailed recommendations, on pages 284-293 of their report, are in effect a development programme for the dismantling of these particular aspects of 'letterism'. The ethnographic study which they include by Cecile Wright, 'School Processes', provides fascinating glimpses of the ways in which the procedures of a school for allocating pupils to streams and sets interact and overlap with aspects of the staffroom culture.

10 How Learners Learn

1   There is a listing of such manuals and handbooks in notes 3-6 in the references below for the essay entitled *Talking As Equals*. Suffice to say here that the genealogy goes back to the development of group dynamics and human relations training in the 1940s and 1950s, and to personal growth and encounter group initiatives in the 1960s. One of the first major handbooks for schools was *Values Clarification* by S. Simon and his co-authors, 1972.

2   This particular exercise is in the handbook *Debate and Decision* (Richardson, Fisher, Flood, 1979). We invented a simple little ranking exercise which involved arranging nine items in a diamond formation, and this has been widely used and copied by others through the 1980s.

3   One seminal author in this respect has of course been Paulo Freire: there are references to his writings in note 5 in the references above for the essay entitled *Learning towards Justice*. His theories of 'dialogue education' or 'problem-posing education' are presented in particular in *Pedagogy of the Oppressed*. Applications of Freire's thinking to mainstream formal education in Western countries have been made by David Kolb and his colleagues based at the Massachusetts Institute of Technology. They situate themselves also in the tradition of group dynamics training developed from about 1945 onwards by Kurt Lewin and his associates. Their theoretical model is a circular one, as is the A-G-E-N-D-A model proposed in this essay, and has been influential on the work of, for example, David Boud and his colleagues in New South Wales, Australia. Broadly similar theories of adult education have also been developed over the years by Malcolm Knowles, who has used in particular the concept of 'andragogy', as distinct from 'pedagogy'. John Codd has defined good educational leadership as 'reflective action', drawing on Paulo Freire amongst others. Carl Rogers in his book *On Personal Power* emphasises various points of convergence between his own methodology in group dynamics and personal growth and the work of Freire. The related concept of Action Learning has been well surveyed with regard

to the training and development of headteachers and other senior staff in schools, by Mike Wallace and his co-authors at the Centre for School Management Training, based at the University of Bristol. The procedures of action research have been applied to equality issues in education in, for example, the project in Berkshire reported by Clem Adelman in *A Fair Hearing for All*. Chris Kyriacou discusses groupwork and experiential learning, and relates these to other kinds of pedagogy, in his overview *Effective Teaching in Schools* (eg, pages 73-77).

4   Andreas Fuglesang is the author of many fascinating publications relating to non-formal adult education in Third World countries, with particular regard to the use of pictorial stimuli of various kinds as a basis for group discussion. The quotations here are from his book *About Understanding*, p.136.

5   On the subject of group learning, as distinct from individual learning, cf Jerome Bruner comparing his present views with those for which he was well-known in the 1960s: 'My model of the child in those days was very much in the tradition of the solo child mastering (sic!) the world by representing it to himself in his own terms. In the intervening years I have come increasingly to recognise that most learning in most settings is a communal activity, a sharing of the culture. . . It is this that leads me to emphasise not only discovery and invention but the importance of negotiating and sharing — in a word, of joint culture creating as an object of schooling. . .' (Bruner,1986, p.127).

6   There is further discussion of problem stories in *Debate and Decision* (Richardson, Fisher, Flood, 1979), and in the article I wrote for the *British Journal of Inservice Education* about the Lesotho workshop which is referred to in this book in the introduction to the essay entitled *Truths about Bias*. (Richardson, 1982)

7   The problems/background/action/values scheme, outlined here in the essay entitled *Learning towards Justice*, provides a useful conceptual approach to the analysis and discussion of problem stories.

8   The 'We Agree Workshop' was developed in the early 1970s by staff at the Charles F Kettering Foundation, Dayton, Ohio. It is described in, for example, the book by Jon Rye Kinghorn and Bill Shaw mentioned later in the list of works cited.

9   These problem stories were largely composed by a team of teachers led by Janet Stuart of the New University of Lesotho, and are reprinted with acknowledgements

11 Talking as Equals

1   This general style of teaching was developed in the United States in the 1960s and came to Britain partly through the field and concerns of personal, social and health education, and partly through world studies, development education and global education.

2   The game 'Getting it Together' is described on page 70 of *Learning for Change in World Society*, 1976, World Studies Project.

3   For example Jill Baldwin's books on *Active Tutorial Work; A Guide to Student-Centred Learning* by Donna Brandes and Paul Ginnis, and *Learning in Action* by Roger Kirk.

4.   For example, Byrne, D. and Rixon, S. *Communication Games.*

5   For example the handbooks developed by the World Studies Project: *Learning for Change in World Society, Debate and Decision*, and *World Studies 8-13* by David Hicks and Simon Fisher. There are also various games and activities in the materials developed by the Centre for Global Education, University of York and the Birmingham Development Education Centre.

6   Many of these phrases are from important and influential books by American authors in this general field. They include: Pfeiffer, J.W. and Jones, J.E. (1970), *Structured Experiences for Human Relations Training*, University Associates Press.

Stanford, G. and B. (1969, *Learning Discussion Skills through Games*, Citation Press.

Wolsk, D. (1975), *An Experience-centred Curriculum*, Unesco.

Simon, S., Howe, K. and Kirschenbaum (1972) *Values Clarification*, Hart Publishing Company.

7   *Education Democracy and Discussion*, (Bridges, 1979)

8   *Political Education and Political Literacy*, by Bernard Crick.

9   *A Language for life* (1975), H.M.S.O. The central arguments of the Bullock Report on learning through talking are emphasised and illustrated also in Barnes's *From Communication to Curriculum* and *Communication and Learning in Small Groups*, by Barnes and Todd.

10   *Lifeskills Teaching Programmes*, by B. Hopson and M. Scally.

11   For a fine academic discussion of the link between interpersonal situations and conceptual learning, see Donaldson, M. (1978), *Children's Minds*, Fontana.

12   Jurgen Habermas's ideas on communicative competence and the ideal speech situation are presented in, for example, Connerton, P., ed. (1976), *Critical Sociology*, Penguin. Other important books on dialogue and democracy written from a neomarxist viewpoint include of course those of Paulo Freire and — very clearly and readably — Brian Wren's *Education for Justice*.

13   Freire, P. *Pedagogy of the Oppressed*.

14   See, for example, Johan Galtung's paper reprinted in Haavelsrud, M., ed. (1975), *Education for Peace*, IPC Technology Press.

15   There is an excellent and very relevant account of teachers' views of pupils in Ing, M., "The Power of Teacher Expectations", in John Twitchin's *Multi-cultural Education: views from the classroom*. In effect (though not explicitly) Ing's article is a plea for more cooperative and horizontal learning in multicutural classrooms.

16   "A growing body of research has shown that students of different races who work together in cooperative learning groups are more likely to have one another as friends than similar students in traditional classrooms." The research is summarised in Hansell, S. and Slavin, R. (1981), "Cooperative Learning and the Structure of Interracial Friendships", *Sociology of Education*, Vol.54 (April 1981).

17   Stig Lindholm *Seeing for Oneself*, Swedish International Development Agency.

18   See for example papers in *Psychology and Race* edited by P. Watson.

19   Attributed to Mahatma Gandhi.

13 Caring and not Caring

1   *River of Compassion*, sub-titled 'a Christian commentary on the Bhagavad Gita', by Bede Griffiths, pages 87 and 88. Elsewhere Griffiths has written : 'Every genuine religion bears witness to some aspect of the divine mystery, embodied in its myths and rituals, in customs and traditions, its prayer and mystical experience... Today we have to open ourselves to the truth in all religions.. This is the hour of trial for Western man. Will he continue to build up his scientific world with nuclear power leading to the devastation of the earth, or will he learn to repent, to turn back, to rediscover the source of life, the wisdom of Mother Earth, which is also the wisdom of the East?' (Griffiths, 1983, p.200)

2   The story is adapted and developed from an idea in *The Song of the Bird* by Antony de Mello, pages 82-83.

3   Quoted from Gandhi's periodical *Harijan* in *The Inner Eye of Love* by William Johnston, p.26.

4   From *Contemplative Prayer* by Thomas Merton, p.141.

5   See for example the articles 'Marching for Jesus' and 'The Church and the State' by Maurice Hobbs and Derek Mitchell respectively, in *Racial Justice*, the excellent journal of Evangelical Christians for Racial Justice, winter 1988. There is fuller and lengthier treatment of this subject in 'The New Religious Right', in Alistair Kee's *Domination or Liberation*.

6   From *The Song of the Bird* by Antony de Mello, p.xvi.

7   From Merton's *Collected Poems*, p.281.

8   *Brideshead Revisited*, p.221 of the Penguin edition.

9   From *The Mirror Mind* by William Johnston, p.174.

10   From *One Minute Wisdom* by Antony de Mello, p.156.

11   Various practical and entirely commonsense approaches to relaxation are described in many books nowadays on stress management. For example, *Pressure at Work ; a survival guide*, by Tanya Arroba and Kim James. Antony de Mello's *Sadhana* is one of the best introductions to relaxation as an essential component of prayer and meditation.

12   Patrick Whitaker, in his excellent compilation *The Learning Process*, includes useful and inspiring practical advice on organising guided fantasies in the mainstream classroom. Visualisation techniques are described in detail in Ferucci's book about psychosynthesis, *What We May Be*, and in Marlene Halpin's little book, *Just Imagine!* Buddhist approaches, entirely adaptable to secular thought-forms, are described attractively by Kathleen McDonald in her *How to Meditate*.

13   There is a detailed account of discussion exercises in the essay in this book entitled *Talking as Equals*, and the notes on this essay include reference to several valuable resource books. One of the clearest recent books on religious storytelling is the one by William Bausch. This is also a marvellous source-book of religious stories, as is also de Mello's *Song of the Bird*.

14   Cited by Iris Murdoch in her secular (but sympathetic) discussion of prayer and religion in *The Sovereignty of Good*, p.59.

15   A seminal text on journalling as an approach to spiritual growth is Ira Progoff's *The Practice of Process Meditation*.

16   Certainly the training of teachers but also quite possibly the education of children and adolescents has much to learn from concepts of 'faith development' and 'personality types', developed from the writings of Jung by, for example, Isobel Myers-Briggs in her *Gifts Differing*. Some of the literature on personality types related to the 'enneagram' also seems promising, for example the 1987 book by Riso.

17   Renee Weber, in her book of conversations and meetings with leading scientists, *Dialogues with Scientists and Sages*, shows at length that mysticism is not irrational. She starts the book with a quotation from Einstein: 'I maintain that the cosmic religious feeling is the strongest and noblest motive for scientific research.' Sir Alister Hardy's research, reported in *The Spiritual Nature of Man*, similarly shows a scientific approach to mystical experience. It is also relevant to note and recall the very hard-headed and down-to-earth approaches to stress management in books such the one cited above (note 11) by Arroba and James: such books are certainly not religious or spiritual in the usual meanings of these terms, but they do take very seriously the approaches to relaxation and visualisation which are frequently commended by explicitly spiritual teachers.

18   This is meditation LX in Tagore's *Gitanjali*, pages 39-40 of the Macmillan of India pocket edition.

14 You Haven't Lost Yet Kids

1   Kit Everard's book on school management is one of the clearest and most accessible distillations of the sound intuitive knowledge which headteachers already have. (Everard,1986). Then also many headteachers find *The Self-Managing School* by Brian Caldwell and Jim Spinks very readable (1988), and that the comprehensive review of research provided by Ken Reid, David Hopkins and Peter Holly in their *Towards the Effective School* is a useful reference guide. One of the clearest and easiest books on general management skills is Madelyn Burley-Allen's *Managing Assertively*.

2   For example, Richard Schmuck itemises the following as the principal norms of staffroom culture in a successful school: direct, open and authentic communication; creative risk-taking to find new ways to solve problems; public discussion on the dynamics of the group itself; and critical assessment of school operations by both staff and students. (In Hopkins and Wideen, eds, 1984, p.30).

3   Courses and Baker Days run according to the A-G-E-N-D-A mnemonic, as outlined in the essay in this book entitled *How Learners Learn,* provide space and security for staff to disagree with each other without destructive conflict or distress.

4   The three terms 'conforming', 'reforming' and 'transforming' are explained further in the essay entitled *Learning towards Justice.*

5   The piece in this book entitled *Bricks in the Wall* is an extended account of the 'structuralist' view of race relations and racism.

6   Marian Fitzgerald's 1987 booklet is a valuable overview of the involvement of black people, and of the place of 'race' issues, in party politics. In a much more journalistic and anecdotal vein, Dervla Murphy provides broadly similar conclusions (Murphy 1987).

7   Modood's 1988 article is extremely well argued on this point of terminology and self-definition.

8   Modood's 1989 article reflecting on Salman Rushdie's *The Satanic Verses* has some interesting and stringent comments about white liberal-agnostic anti-racists.

9   See, for example, John Richmond's book on classroom language.

10   Caldwell and Spinks, *op cit* (note 1 above) include an excellent chapter on formal policies and policy statements in individual schools, pages 89-107.

11   Reprinted in Holt's *The Underachieving School*, pages 15-34. Holt refers to 'these dull, ugly and inhuman places, where nobody ever says anything either very true or truthful, where everybody is playing a kind of role, as in a charade. . . ' (Page 28).

12   On stress management two of the friendliest books readily available are those by Madelyn Burley-Allen (note 1 above) and *Pressure at Work: a survival guide*, by Tanya Arroba and Kim James.

15 Worth the Paper it's Written On?

1   Basic readings on systems thinking are provided in the compilation edited by F.E.Emery, 1969. Systems thinking has been applied specifically to the study of local government by Robert Haynes, who commends it not only as a conceptual approach to understanding local government but also as a way of encouraging local government organisations to be more open and responsive to their environments.

2   A focus on the systemic distribution of resources has been a hallmark of Julian Le Grand's writings, for example *The Strategy of Equality: redistribution and the social services*, 1982. 'Almost all public expenditure on the social services,' he writes, 'benefits the better off to a greater extent than the poor. In all the relevant areas, there persist substantial inequalities in public expenditure, in use, in opportunity, in access and in outcome.' (p.3). With regard to primary education he notes that 'the top socio-economic group (professionals, employers and managers) receives nearly 50% more public expenditure on education per person in the relevant age group than the bottom group (semi and unskilled manual workers). . . twice as much for secondary pupils over 16, over 3 times as much for further education and over 5 times as much for university education. . . These inequalities have remained largely constant over the last 50 years.' (p. 75).

3   An organisation's mental framework is sometimes known as its 'appreciative system' or 'disposition'. It is reflected and maintained in organisational culture and structures rather than in formal policy statements, but the latter do at best have their role and influence. Ken Young and Naomi Connelly write thus about dispositions in local government: "Dispositions may best be understood as very general and taken-for-granted assumptions about both the facts of a situation and its evaluation. Within a broad corpus of more or less consistent assumptions certain phenomena, relationships, qualities and values are held to be self-evident. Certain other issues, if they present themselves, are held to be undiscussable.' (Young and Connelly, 1981, p. 158).The struggles around the Berkshire policy statement through the 1980s were very much to do with what is, and is not, discussable — for example, and in particular, whether structural racism is discussable.

4   For example, the Swann Report came in for much hammering from professional philosophers, who criticised it with very little awareness and appreciation that it represented a negotiation between conflicting ideologies and interests : see *Education for a Pluralist Society* (Haynes, 1987).

5   The Berkshire policy papers were published as the first annex in the Swann Report, pages 366 onwards. Their concept of structural racism is explicated further in the essay in this book on 'letterism', *Bricks in the Wall.*

6   From 'East Coker' in *Four Quartets*, p.21 of the Faber edition.

16 Believing Enough?

1   Sarah del Tufo, Lawrence Randle and John Ryan, 'Inequality in a School System', in A. Ohri et alia, eds, *Community Work and Racism*, p.84.

2   Wendy Robinson, *Exploring Silence*, p.8.

3   Paulo Freire, *Pedagogy of the Oppressed*, p.119.

4   Salman Rushdie, *Midnight's children.*

5   Chris Mullard, 'The State's Response to Racism: towards a relational explanation', in A. Ohri et alia, eds, p.57.

6   E.M. Forster, *A Passage to India*, the last sentence.

7   David Lodge, *Small World.*

8   Martin Buber, *Tales of the Hasidim* quoted by Wendy Robinson, op cit, p.4.

9   Thomas Merton, *No Man is an Island* p.278.

10   Alice Walker, *Horses Make a Landscape Look More Beautiful*, p76.

List of Works Cited

Adelman, C, ed, (1982) *A Fair Hearing for All* Reading : Bulmershe Research Publications

Angelou, Maya (1987) *All God's Children Need Travelling Shoes* London: Virago Press

Arroba, T and James, K (1987) *Pressure at Work: a Survival Guide* London: McGraw Hill

Ashley, B (1978) *A Kind of Wild Justice* Oxford: Clarendon Press

Baldwin, James (1963) *The Fire Next Time* London: Michael Joseph

Baldwin, J and Wells, H (1979/1981) *Active Tutorial Work Books 1-5* Oxford: Basil Blackwell

Bausch, W (1984) Storytelling: *Imagination and Faith* Mystic Connecticut: Twenty Third Publications

Berger, P and Kellner, H (1971) 'Marriage and the Construction of Reality' in Cosin, B et alia (eds) op cit.

Berkshire County Council (1983) *Education for Racial Equality: General Policy*, reprinted in the Committee of Inquiry's *Education for All*, op cit, pp.366-370

Berry, James, ed (1981) *Bluefoot Traveller* London: Harrap

Biko, S (1978) *I Write What I Like* London: Heinemann

Blackmore, J (1989) 'Educational Leadership: A Feminist Critique and Reconstruction' in Smyth, J (ed) op cit.

Boud, D., Keogh, R. and Walker, D. (1985) 'Promoting Reflection in Learning: a Model' and 'What is Reflection in Learning ?' in the same authors' book *Reflection: Turning Experience into Learning* London : Kogan Page.

219

Boud, D. and Griffin, V. (eds) (1987) *Appreciating Adults Learning* London: Kogan Page.

Boyd, W. (1987) *The New Confessions* London: Hamish Hamilton

Brecht, B (1981) *Poems* 1913-1956 London: Eyre Methuen.

Brandes, D and Ginnis, P (1986) *Guide to Student-Centred Learning* Oxford: Basil Blackwell.

Brent Education Department (1987) *Equality and Excellence* London

Briggs Myers, I. (1980) *Gifts Differing* Palo Alto California : Consulting Psychologists Press

Bridges, D (1979) *Education, Democracy and Discussion* Slough : NFER Publishing Company

Brown, C (1975) *Literacy in 30 Hours : Paulo Freire's Process in North East Brazil* London: Writers and Readers Publishing Cooperative

Bruner, J (1986) *Actual Minds, Possible Worlds* Cambridge Massachusetts: Harvard University Press

Burley-Allen, M (1983) *Managing Assertively* London: John Wiley.

Byrne, D and Rixon, S (1979) *Communication Games* Slough: NFER Publishing Company

Caldwell, B and Spinks, J (1988) *The Self-Managing School* Lewes: The Falmer Press

Carriere, J-L and Brook, P (1988) *The Mahabharata* London: Methuen

Centre for Contemporary Cultural Studies (1982) *The Empire Strikes Back* London: Hutchinson

Chapman, R and Rutherford, J (eds) (1988) *Male Order: unwrapping masculinity* London : Lawrence and Wishart

Codd, J (1989) 'Educational Leadership as Reflective Action' in Smyth, J, op cit.

Cohen, P and Gardner, C (1982) *It Aint Half Racist Mum* London: Comedia Publishing Group

Committee of Inquiry into the Education of Children from Ethnic Minority Groups (1985) *Education for All* (The Swann Report) London: Her Majesty's Stationery Office
Cosin, B et alia, eds, (1971) *School and Society* London: Routledge and Open University Press

Cummings, E.E (1960) *Selected Poems* London: Faber

de Mello, A. (1984) *Sadhana : Christian Exercises in Eastern Form* New York: Image Books

de Mello, A. (1984) *The Song of the Bird* New York: Image Books

de Mello, A (1985) *One Minute Wisdom* Anand India: Gujarat Sahitya Prakash

del Tufo, S, Randle, L, Ryan,J (1982) 'Inequality in a School System' in Ohri, A et alia, eds, op cit.

Desai, A. (1978) *Games at Twilight* London: Heinemann

Edgar, D (1987) 'Dreams of the Volk', *New Socialist* 18, January 1987

Eggleston, J, Dunn, D and Anjali, M (1986) *Education for Some,* Stoke on Trent: Trentham Books

Emery, F (ed) (1969) *Systems Thinking* Harmondsworth : Penguin

Everard, K (1986) *Developing Management in Schools* Oxford: Basil Blackwell

Ferguson, M (1980) *The Aquarian Conspiracy: personal and social transformation in the 1980s* London: Routledge and Kegan Paul

Ferucci, P (1982) *What We May Be: the Visions and Techniques of Psychosynthesis* Wellingborough: Turnstone Press

Fitzgerald, M (1987) *Black People and Party Politics in Britain* London: The Runnymede Trust

Forster, E M (1951) *Two Cheers for Democracy,* reprinted as *I Believe* in Auden, W H et al (1962) *Nineteen Personal Philosphies* London: Allen and Unwin

Forster, E M (1924) *A Passage to India*

Fox, M. and Swimme, B. (1982) *Manifesto for a Global Civilisation* Santa Fe New Mexico: Bear and Company

Fox, M. (1983) *Original Blessing : a Primer in Creation Spirituality* Santa Fe New Mexico: Bear and Company

Freire, P. (1972) *Pedagogy of the Oppressed* Harmondsworth : Penguin Books

Freire, P (1976) *Education: The Practice of Freedom* London: Writers and Readers Publishing Cooperative

Freire, P. (1978) *Pedagogy in Process: the letters to Guinea-Bissau* London: Writers and Readers Publishing Cooperative

Fuglesang, A. (1982) *About Understanding: Ideas and Observations on Cross-Cultural Communication* Uppsala Sweden : Dag Hammarskjold Foundation

Galtung, J (1973) *The European Community: a superpower in the making* London: Allen and Unwin.

Goldsmiths Media Research Group (1987) *Media Coverage of London Councils* London: Goldsmiths College

Griffiths, B. (1982) *The Marriage of East and West* London: William Collins

Griffiths, B. (1987) *River of Compassion; a Christian Commentary on the Bhagavad Gita* New York: Amity Press

Halpin, M. (1982) *Imagine That! — Using Phantsy in Spiritual Direction* Dubuque Iowa: Wm C Brown Company

Hansell, S and Slavin, R (1981) 'Co-operative Learning and the Structure of Inter-racial Friendships' *Sociology of Education* Vol 54 (April)

Hardy, A. (1979) *The Spiritual Nature of Man: a study of contemporary religious experience* Oxford University Press

Harrison, Tony (1984) *Selected Poems* Harmdondsworth: Penguin Books

Hawkins, E (1984) *Awareness of Language: an Introduction* Cambridge University Press

Haynes, R (1980) *Organisation Theory and Local Government* London: Allen and Unwin

Heider, J (1986) *The Tao of Leadership,* Aldershot: Wildwood Press

Hobbs, M (1988) 'Marching for Jesus', *Racial Justice* winter 1988, no. 10.

Hodge, J., Struckmann, D. and Trost, L. (1975) *Cultural Bases of Racism and Group Oppression* Berkeley California: Two Riders Press

Holt, J. (1971) *The Underachieving School* London: Pitman

Hopkins, D and Wideen, M (1984) *Alternative Perspectives on School Improvement* Lewes: The Falmer Press

Hopson, B and Scally, M (1980) *Lifeskills Teaching Programmes* Leeds: Lifeskills Associates

Humphrey, N and Lifton. R (1984) *In a Dark Time* London: Faber

Ing, M (1981) 'The Power of Teacher Expectations' in Twitchin, J op cit (1981)

Iyer, R (1978) *The Moral and Political Thought of Mahatma Gandhi* Oxford: The Clarendon Press

Jenkins, J (1987) 'The Green Sheep in Colonel Gadaffi Drive', *New Statesman*, 9 January 1987.

Johnston, W (1981) *The Mirror Mind* London: William Colins

Joseph, K (1984) Speech at Reading London: DES press release

Kee, A (1986) *Domination or Liberation: the place of religion in social conflict* London: SCM Press

Kelly, E and Cohn, T (1988) *Racism in Schools: New Research Evidence* Stoke on Trent: Trentham Books

King, Martin Luther (1963) *Why We Can't Wait* New York: Signet Books

Kinghorn, J and Shaw, W (1977) *Handbook for Global Education: a Working Manual* Dayton Ohio: Kettering Foundation

Kirk, R (1987) *Learning in Action: Activities for Personal and Group Development* Oxford: Basil Blackwell

Knowles, M (1984) *The Adult Learner : a Neglected Species* Houston Texas: Gulf

Kolb, D and Fry, R (1975) 'Towards an Applied Theory of Experiential Learning' in Cooper, C (ed) *Theories of Group Processes* Chichester : John Wiley

Kyriacou, C (1986) *Effective Teaching in Schools* Oxford: Basil Blackwell

Lindholm, S (1975) *Seeing for Oneself* Stockholm: Swedish International Development Agency

Lodge, David (1985) *Small World* Harmondsworth : Penguin Book

Lovelock, J (1979) *Gaia — a New Look at Life on Earth* Oxford: the Clarendon Press

Mansfield, K (1922) *The Garden Party* Harmondsworth: Penguin Books

McDonald, K (1984) *How to Meditate: a Practical Guide* London: Wisdom Books

Merton, T (1957) *No Man Is An Island* New York : Dell Publishing

Merton, T (1973) *Contemplative Prayer* London: Darton Longman and Todd

Mitchell, D (1988) 'The Church and the State in Britain', *Racial Justice* winter 1988, no.10.

Modood, T (1988) '"Black", Racial Equality and Asian Identity' *New Community* Vol XIV No 3 London: Commission for Racial Equality

Modood, T (1989) 'Alabama Britain' London: *The Guardian* 22 May

Mullard, C (1982) 'The State's Response to Racism : towards a relational explanation, in Ohri, A et al, op cit

Murdoch, I (1970) *The Sovereignty of Good* London: Routledge and Kegan Paul

Murphy, D (1987) *Tales from Two Cities : travel of another sort* London : John Murray

Murray, N and Searle, C (1989) *Racism and the Press in Thatcher's Britain* London: Institute of Race Relations

Ngugi Wa Thiong'o (1977) *Petals of Blood* London: Heinemann

Ohri, A, Manning, B and Curno, P (Eds) *Community Work and Racism* London: Routledge and Kegan Paul

Pfeiffer, J and Jones, J (1970) *Structured Experiences for Human Relations Training* University Associates Press

Progoff I (1980) *The Practice of Process Meditation* New York : Dialogue House

Reid, K, Hopkins, D and Holly, P (1987) *Towards the Effective School* Oxford : Basil Blackwell

Richardson,R, Fisher, S, Flood,M (1979) *Debate and Decision : schools in a world of change* London : One World Trust

Richardson, R (1982) 'Beyond the Walls: a case study', *British Journal of Inservice Education*, autumn 1982, vol 9 no 1

Richmond, J (1982) *The Resources of Classroom Language* London: Edward Arnold

Riso, D (1987) *Personality Types: Using the Enneagram for Self-Discovery* Boston: Houghton Mifflin

Robinson, W (1974) *Exploring Silence* Oxford: SLG Press

Rogers, C (1978) *On Personal Power* London: Constable

Roszak, T (1976) *Unfinished Animal : the Aquarian Frontier and the Evolution of Consciousness* London: Faber

Roth, P (1983) *The Anatomy Lesson* London: Jonathan Cape

Rushdie, S (1981) *Midnight's Children* London: Jonathan Cape

Rushdie, S (1987) *The Jaguar Smile* London: Pan Books

Sharron, H (1987) *Changing Children's Minds: Feuerstein's Revolution in the Teaching of Intelligence* London: Souvenir Press

Schumacher, E (1973) *Small is Beautiful* London: Blond and Briggs

Schwarz, W and D (1987) *Breaking Through* Bideford: Green Books

Sheldrake, R (1987) *A New Science of Life* London: Paladin

Simon, S, Howe, K and Kirschenbaum, H (1972) *Values Clarification* New York: Hart Publishing Company

Sivanandan, A (1983) 'Challenging Racism: strategies for the '80s' London: *Race and Class* Volume XXV Number 2

Smith, W (1976) *The Meaning of Conscientizao: the Goal of Paulo Freire's Pedagogy* University of Massachusetts Press

Smyth, J (1989) *Critical Perspectives on Educational Leadership* Lewes: The Falmer Press

Starhawk (1982) *Dreaming the Dark : Magic, Sex and Politics* Boston Mass: Beacon Books

Tagore, R (1913) *Gitanjali* Madras India: Macmillan Company

Thornton, M (1984) *Spiritual Direction: a Practical Introduction* London: SPCK

Twitchin, J (1981) *Multicultural Education: Views from the Classroom* London: BBC Publications

Twitchin, J (1988) *The Black and White Media Book : Handbook for the Study of Racism and Television* Stoke on Trent : Trentham Books

Walker, Alice (1985) *Horses Make a Landscape Look More Beautiful* London: The Womens Press

Wallace, M, Bailey, J and Kirk, P (1988) *Action Learning: practice and potential in school management development* Bristol : National Development Centre for School Management Training

Weber. R (1986) *Dialogues with Scientists and Sages: the Search for Unity* London: Routledge and Kegan Paul

Whitaker, P (1984) *The Learning Process* York : World Studies Teacher Training Centre

Wolsk, D (1975) *An Experience-Centred Curriculum* Paris: Unesco

World Studies Project (1976) *Learning for Change in World Society* London: One World Trust

Wren, B (1977) *Education for Justice* London: SCM Press

Young, K and Connelly, N (1981) *Policy and Practice in the Multi-Racial City* London : Policy Studies Institute

Zukav, G (1979) *The Dancing Wu Li Masters: an Overview of the New Physics* London : Rider/Hutchinson